Schools and the Changing World

Schools and the Changing World:
Struggling Toward the Future

Benjamin Levin and J. Anthony Riffel

RoutledgeFalmer
Taylor & Francis Group

LONDON AND NEW YORK

First published in 1997
By Routledge Falmer
11 New Fetter Lane, London EC4P 4EE

Transferred to Digital Printing 2004

A catalogue record for this book is available from the British Library

ISBN 0-7507-0662-7 cased
ISBN 0-7507-0617-1 paper

Library of Congress Cataloging-in-Publication Data are available on request

Jacket design by Caroline Archer

Typeset in 10/12 pt, Garamond by
Graphicraft Typesetters Ltd., Hong Kong.

Contents

Contents

Acknowledgments

The research on which this book is based was supported by grants from the Social Sciences and Humanities Research Council of Canada. We thank many people for their help in conducting the research and in writing this book. Our research colleagues — Nancy Buchanan, Antoinette Van Kuik and Professor Anthony Ezeife of the University of Uyo in Nigeria — all made important contributions to the study. Our colleagues in educational administration — John Long, Hal May, John Stapleton and Jonathan Young — provide the kind of support and stimulation one hopes for from colleagues. Our Department Head — Romulo Magsino — and department secretary — Pat Draho — were helpful at all times. Many colleagues in education in Manitoba and elsewhere provided data of various kinds and helped us work through the issues in the course of seminars, meetings and informal discussions. Comments from academic colleagues and anonymous journal reviewers of papers related to this project have also helped us clarify our thinking. Much of the writing was done while on study leave from The University of Manitoba and we thank the Institute of Education at the University of Cambridge, England, for its support as well as many British colleagues who participated in seminars related to this work.

Most of all we thank our colleagues in the five partner school districts for accepting us into their organizations, and for their candor and willingness to reflect on their views and practices. We can't claim that we speak for them — a complex question that we take up in Chapter 2 — but we have learned a great deal from them. Of course all opinions, errors and weaknesses are solely the responsibility of the authors.

A somewhat different version of Chapter 6 is in press in *Interchange*.

A somewhat different version of Chapter 7 is in press in *Educational Management and Administration*.

A somewhat different version of Chapter 9 is in press in the 1997 Politics of Education Yearbook, *Mapping Shifting Professional and Community Relationships*, edited by Jane Clark Lindle and Maureen McClure, to be published by Falmer Press.

Why Another Book on Educational Change?

This book is about the ways in which school systems try to cope with social change. We believe that changes in social and economic conditions — for example income distribution, work opportunities for graduates, family structures, gender roles or information technology — have important implications for the way schooling is conducted. Although these changes are, in our view, vital to the future of education, most research on school change has focused on the internal dynamics of school systems — on such matters as implementing new curricula or improving teaching practices or assessment procedures. Relatively little empirical or theoretical work addresses the ways that school systems respond to social change.

This book is the product of a program of research aimed at an improved understanding of how school systems understand and respond to a rapidly changing world. Educators are highly aware of the powerful impact of social change, and generally see such changes as making their work more difficult. There is no doubt that changes in many areas are making traditional practices problematic. However we argue that school systems do not have in place adequate processes for learning about, understanding and developing responses to changes in the larger society. In terms of understanding, sources of information are limited, learning processes tend to be informal and ad hoc, and opportunities to talk about the meaning of social change are not sufficient. In terms of responding, school systems rely primarily on extensions of existing activities and practices. Even though we believe that many social changes pose fundamental challenges to the current mode of schooling, it appears that school systems are not generally taking a long-term or strategic approach in responding to change, and are not sufficiently engaged in a process of experimentation and learning in order to cope with new challenges and problems.

Our principal colleagues in this research were elected officials and senior administrators in a Canadian province and especially in five school districts in that province. We use the term 'colleagues' deliberately because we tried to frame our research as a mutual enterprise with the participating districts.

Our colleagues were perceptive, had a good grasp of their school systems, and were committed to improving education. They also believe that the work of schools is affected by a wide variety of demographic, economic, technological and social changes and acknowledge that, despite their efforts, their responses are not sufficient. Partly this is because the problems they face are extremely difficult and complex, and extend far beyond the traditional mandate of the schools. Many of our colleagues feel uncertainty about the purposes of schooling in the light of changing conditions.

While acknowledging these very real constraints, we also feel that school systems create some of their own difficulties. The ideas, structures and processes which frame and shape their efforts are essentially inward looking and limiting. Social changes surrounding schools raise fundamental questions about the established purposes and organization of schools, as well as the nature and processes of education, but we did not see many signs that people's school districts had become engaged with such questions. Understanding change requires approaches to learning, analysis and experimentation but these are seldom an established part of the operation of school systems.

In noting what we regard as insufficiencies in current practice we are not trying to criticize our colleagues, but to point to possibilities that all of us could see as helpful. The intellectual and organizational change of learning to think and do education differently is very demanding. Understanding and responding to social change in educationally appropriate ways will require a lot of determination, resourcefulness and political skill. It involves challenging much of what now passes for common sense. We'll need new ways of thinking about schools and their relationships to other social processes and institutions: thinking about schools *and* social change, not *versus* social change, which is now the more common stance. While a more formal approach to understanding and responding to social change will be helpful, the greater need is for practical imagination to help create the required practices and structures. And all this has to happen despite criticism, budget cuts and top–down directives. The challenge is enormous.

Organization and Use of the Book

Our hope is that the book will give educators, researchers, and those directly involved in schools some helpful ideas for their work. For researchers, we believe we have provided a different view of issues of change, perhaps distinctive approaches to some central problems (such as organizational learning) and data that help illuminate these questions. Our focus on the importance of external change is, we believe, an important addition to valuable work already done on the internal dynamics of change.

We hope that educators in school systems may find here ideas that will help them reflect on their own situations and activities — a way of looking at the 'big picture' that is so important and also so elusive. If we have succeeded, readers will find our analysis thought-provoking and stimulating, even where you may disagree with our approach. We have tried to strike a balance in our use of the literature, providing enough references that the reader can see the sources of our data and ideas and track those that may be of interest, but also keeping the book readable and avoiding so many parenthetical references that they interfere with reading.

Although we draw primarily on empirical work from Canada, we believe that examining these ideas and experiences can help all those interested in education to do a better job of responding to change. Our experience talking with colleagues from other countries — the United States, Britain, Israel, Hong Kong, Nigeria, and elsewhere — as well as our reading of the literature, suggest that although the specific situations differ, schools everywhere are faced with the challenge of understanding and responding to change in the larger society, and are struggling with this task. To make the international links clearer, we cite research from Britain and the United States as well as from Canada in our discussion of many of the issues in the book.

In Chapter 2 we describe our research and address the problems we encountered in trying to do research which was critical of existing practice but also intended to be helpful to people in schools. It is important for us to point out that though we rely on the data from our colleagues in schools in framing our analysis, they would not necessarily agree with the views we express; we discuss this issue in the section of Chapter 2 on 'two-column research'.

Chapter 3 contains a fuller discussion of the nature of social change and its implications for schools. We provide the context for the research and give a description of the five school districts which were our partners in this enquiry. In this chapter we also describe the range of social changes that our colleagues in the school districts identified, and say something about the ways in which issues were identified and talked about.

Chapter 4 analyses the general processes of learning about social change. We ask what educators think about a changing world and where their images and ideas come from. Drawing on a relevant literature from several fields and using data from the five school districts and our broader sample of administrators and policy-makers we illustrate the ways in which issues do or do not get noticed, defined, and translated into action.

Chapter 5 is a similar discussion of responding to social change. What strategies are schools and school systems using to try to cope with the changes they see as important? What factors shape these strategies and limit other options?

In Chapters 6 through 10 we discuss five specific issues that illustrate the general problems of learning and responding to social change. The issues are: change in the labour force (Chapter 6), changes in information technology (Chapter 7), child poverty (Chapter 8), changes in families (Chapter 9), and changes in political processes (Chapter 10). We use each issue to extend the more general discussion of Chapters 4 and 5 by illustrating the different ways in which particular issues are thought about and taken up. In each chapter we discuss the perceptions of our colleagues about the issue, their sources of knowledge, and the strategies they say they are pursuing to try to deal with the issue. We supplement what we learned from our colleagues in the case study districts with data from interviews with, and surveys of, a broader set of educators in the same province. The first three of these chapters — labour force, technology, and poverty — are somewhat more extensive because they formed a larger part in our original research design.

The final chapter presents some of our suggestions and recommendations for schools and school systems. The dilemmas we raise have no magic answers. We don't offer 'six ways to become a learning organization' or 'four steps to effective strategic planning'. Few such proposals are worth much, since they ignore the real constraints and cultures that organizations must live with. We do put forward proposals that we believe would be helpful, and are feasible in most school systems. If we expect perfection we are almost certain to be disappointed, but there is much that can be done even given all the difficulties; on this score we remain optimistic.

Chapter 1

Social Change and Organizational Response

How schools cope with a world of change is clearly an issue of fundamental importance. People will agree that schools need to change, even if they agree on nothing else (such as what changes are needed, why, and how they can be brought about).

In this book we discuss the ways that schools and school systems learn about the changing world around them and the way they try to respond to the changes they see as important. The changes we are concerned with are those lying outside the school itself — such matters as economic, social, political, technological or demographic shifts. As we will show a little later, real and lasting changes in education have been driven much more by external factors of this kind than they have by the planned change efforts of educators or policy-makers. A very wide range of such matters can affect the work of schooling. Our interest is in how those effects occur.

The two ideas, of 'learning' and 'responding', are both critical to our analysis. Simply studying what people believe or know is insufficient, because although action is related to people's ideas, the relationship is not a simple one; people don't always behave consistently with what they claim to know. On the other hand, to study action without attention to ideas and beliefs seems to us pointless, since we do live in a world in which ideas and intentions matter. Somewhere between learning and responding is the rather fuzzy idea of knowing; 'knowing' not in the limited sense we usually use in schools and universities, but knowing something in a way that makes it part of everyday consciousness and shapes actions as well as ideas.

Although these issues are vital, they have not been the subject of very much empirical enquiry in education. Much has been written — we discuss some of the literature later in this chapter — about what schools *should do* in response to social change; much less work has been done to describe what schools *actually do* about these matters. Our intent is to use a solid base of empirical evidence to discuss both questions.

Our basic proposition is straightforward: though schools are being driven by external changes, they are not well organized to optimize either their learning about change or their response to it. It isn't that schools are unchanging or unwilling to change; the problem has to do with the mismatch between the scale of the challenge and the skills, practices and resources we currently bring to bear on it.

So boldly put, the argument hides a myriad of complexities. Before plunging into this subject, however, we examine some of what has been written about schools and their response to change.

Views on Social Change

It is a truism to say that we live in a world of change. Indeed, we are bombarded with messages about the pervasiveness and importance of changes in our natural, social, economic and technological environments. These discussions range from the popularisers, such as Naisbitt (1990), Ogden (1993) or Toffler and Toffler (1995), to the management theorists, such as Drucker (1992), Vaill (1989) or Handy (1994), to more philosophical or theoretical discussions such as those of Giddens (1994) or Taylor (1991). Some of these analyses focus on discrete areas of change — for example, an ageing population, degradation of the natural environment, increased focus on human rights. Others take a broader view, talking about larger scale systemic changes. Some theorists see our society changing in quite fundamental ways. Postmodernism is one term in current use, though in many different ways; Hargreaves (1994) uses the term 'postmodernity' to distinguish a social situation from an intellectual viewpoint (which is his analysis of postmodernism). Giddens (1994) uses the term 'high modernity' to stress connections between present and past more than differences, while Taylor (1991) speaks of the 'malaise of modernity'. What these and similar analyses have in common is a much broader view of social change, one that sees important shifts underway in fundamental constituting elements of a society such as concepts of identity, approaches to politics, legitimating structures, and epistemological underpinnings.

Although much of this larger literature is not readily accessible to educators, one doesn't have to look very hard to find discussions of the implications of external change for schools. Typically the authors of work on education reform will begin by noting various changes in the larger society that are — or should be — affecting the work of schools. For example, Dennison (1988) lists four 'dominant factors' — 'the reorganisation of the productive processes', increasing pressure from the public, restraints on government expenditure, and 'the emergence of high technology in the classroom'. Henchey (1988) lists changing knowledge, communications technology, convergence of work and learning, growing complexity, and increasing pluralism as key challenges for education. A recent OECD report cites globalization and ageing populations; widely diffused information technologies; changes in the organization of work and changing values as related to the creation of 'post-industrial' society (OECD, 1995, p. 4).

Other work in education focuses on the importance of single changes and their implications. For example, most of the current rhetoric around school reform is based on an economic rationale. The task of schools is seen as being to prepare students to fill an economic role variously related to terms such as productivity, competitiveness, and entrepreneurship. The future prosperity of our society is claimed to be critically dependent on how well schools do this task. Many government reports and policies as well as those of business organizations have been based on this view.

Another analysis sees schools as needing to respond to increasing social diversity — in ethnicity, gender, religion, or class — although among those who see diversity as the critical factor affecting schools there are vehement disagreements on remedies. Some (e.g., Holmes, 1992) take the view that a common school is not possible, and we must therefore allow different groups to develop and maintain their own schools and school systems. Others (e.g., Cummins, 1988; Troyna, 1993) see schools as acting to perpetuate inequalities of various kinds, and advocate multicultural or anti-racist education in an attempt to build an integrated school system that values different groups equally.

Andy Hargreaves has been one of the commentators on changing external forces and their impacts on schools who has adopted a broader view and also related it to the day-to-day realities of teaching and learning without being simplistic. His 1994 book *Changing Teachers, Changing Times* has an extended discussion of specific elements of social change and their implications for schools. Hargreaves cites seven key areas of change, all of which affect the needs of students and the situation of schools: the flexible economy; globalization; the decline of certainty in knowledge; the need for organizations that are less rigidly structured; changes in people's sense of self and the increasing pressure on individuals to define and create themselves (an analysis developed more fully in Giddens, 1994); the growth of technological imagery and simulation; and the compression of time and space. He notes that all of these trends contain inconsistencies and contradictions. They do not lead us forward in some direct way to a new world, but make it increasingly important for people to shape their own futures. In a later article, Hargreaves (1995) further develops some of these paradoxes — for example that many parents have given up responsibility for the things they appear to value most; that businesses don't use the skills they demand schools produce; or that globalization is also leading to increased tribalism.

Not everyone accepts that change is as pervasive as Hargreaves suggests. Beniger (1986) has identified more than fifty different claimed 'transformations' of society since 1945, suggesting that our readiness to embrace grand schemes of change may be greater than the changes themselves. Historical change typically occurs over long periods of time, as confirmed by the expert who, when asked to identify the main results of the fall of the Roman Empire noted that it was still too soon to tell! On the other hand, human life is also subject to sharp and unexpected discontinuities, whether natural disasters or surprising events created by humans. As Dror (1986) puts it,

> There is a high objective probability of low-probability events occurring frequently. In subjective terms, surprise dominates. (Dror, 1986, p. 168)

And Nickerson (1992) makes a similar case.

> My sense is that, especially during recent years, we have been more often surprised by the ways in which technological advances have out-distanced our imaginations than by the ways they have lagged behind them. In any case, if the past gives us any clues at all as to what the future holds, the one thing that we can be quite sure of is that there will be surprises . . . some of the most significant developments are very likely to be those that no one foresees. (Nickerson, 1992, p. 6)

So, although there is little agreement on the precise nature and shape of social change, educators are likely to continue to experience pressures from such changes. Still, a large portion of work on education change and reform continues to focus on the internal dynamics of the school, not its external relationships and situation. The discussion of change often proceeds as if the school were in charge of its own destiny and could itself determine what was to be done. Many of the leading books on education change and reform have little to say about social context and its implications for education. If these are mentioned it is typically in passing at the beginning as a measure of the urgency of change.

The Paradox of School Change

If educators have a surplus of anything, it is advice. It seems everyone has an opinion about schools — perhaps because everyone has gone to school and knows something about them. Both the popular and academic literature are full of ideas about what is wrong with schools and how to improve them (and this book adds to the collection!). The advice is sweeping and not always consistent. Schools, we are told, need to teach critical thinking, or to renew emphasis on basic skills, or both. Schools need to deal with the realities of modern life for young people, or to instill firmer discipline. Schools need to work more closely with parents, or to become more professional organizations. Schools need to become mini-communities, or require the alleged discipline of market forces. Schools need more options, or fewer options, or different options. Schools should be more autonomous, or more closely regulated by government. And so on.

Allied to the barrage of advice is the argument that schools have not changed very much. Schools are often accused of failing to keep pace with social change. School systems are described as still organized largely on the nineteenth century lines which characterized their beginnings.

> The age-graded, centrally controlled and highly bureaucratized system of public schools has survived largely in the form in which it was

invented in the late nineteenth century. Virtually all of the successful changes in the system could be classified as those that helped the system to expand, to extend its services or to become more efficient. (Grant and Murray, 1996, p. 93)

Schools are also said to be highly resistant to change. In an oft-cited piece, Larry Cuban (1988) writes, 'so much school reform has taken place over the last century yet schooling appears to be pretty much the same as it has always been' (p. 341). One could cite dozens of examples of the same argument. The consequences are sometimes framed in almost apocalyptic terms:

Certainly the environmental forces which public school officials once were able to contain, and the conflict the institution was once able to channel or suppress now appear to be overwhelming it . . . If that continues to be the case, the fate of the institution of public schooling will be determined largely by forces in the societal and institutional environment . . . (Cibulka, 1996, p. 20)

Still others accuse schools of changing too much and too frequently; of being prey to every fad or bandwagon that comes along (e.g., Slavin, 1990). According to these critics, new tasks are assigned, new curricula developed, new methods of teaching proposed, and new organization forms are introduced too often. Changes are adopted and then abandoned with a startling frequency, and many of those that are put into practice are said to be badly thought out and have pernicious consequences.

Although these claims seem contradictory, each also appears to have some validity. When we compare schools with other organizations, they do seem remarkably stable in their basic organization and operation. In many other settings basic changes have occurred in the nature of staffing and the roles of staff, the basic technology being used, the physical structure, and the organization of resources. Hospitals have become intensive users of technology. Much banking now occurs at instant teller machines nowhere near an actual bank. Industrial settings use more equipment and fewer people. But most schools today would be pretty recognizable even to someone who hadn't set foot in one for decades. They are still organized around the agricultural calendar and the six hour day. They still revolve around classes of children, grouped by age or subject, being taught by a single adult. Paper, pens, and the chalkboard — now sometimes white, to be sure — are still the basic technologies. Grades, textbooks, examinations, marks, detentions, extra-curricular activities — all seem remarkably similar to past practice.

Some problems or issues also seem to be continuous. One can easily cite many examples of issues that have been the subject of debate in schools for decades, such as the relationship between schools and work, programming for students not planning to go on to post-secondary education, grouping practices in the elementary grades, retention in grade and so on.

That stability, however, is far from the whole story. The experience of many educators over the last twenty years is one of continuous change, often externally imposed, and soon succeeded by further change. The complaint of many in school systems is not that there have been too few changes but that there have been too many. The progressive movement of the 1960s was replaced by the 'back to basics' of the 1970s and early 1980s, followed by a whole variety of other movements — accountability, increased testing, reduced funding, changes in curriculum requirements, reorganization of schools from primary and secondary to early, middle, and senior (or vice-versa), changes in the organization of the school year (moving to semesters or moving away from semesters), changes in the school schedule (from 40 minute classes to 80 minute classes and back again), reductions in numbers or powers of school districts and local authorities, requirements for school-based planning, requirements for parental councils, parental choice of schools, and so on. The entire apparatus of special education — the idea that schools can and should be effective with students with a wide variety of handicapping conditions — is only about thirty years old. Learning disabilities, mainstreaming, multiply-disabled children, individual education programs — all these substantive issues of today were essentially unknown until the late 1960s. Attention to differences in gender, ethnicity, language, sexual preference and social class have brought a new series of issues around how we reconcile respect for difference with some sense of commonality (Riffel, Levin and Young, 1996). Technology has become yet another major focus of change as schools develop computer capacities and curricula. The idea of teachers as professionals, changes in labour relations, and increased certification requirements have made an important difference to schools. And let us not forget the constant additions to the work of school — sex education, drug education, conflict mediation, values and character building, life skills, and so on.

The changes have intensified in the last five to ten years, driven increasingly by the efforts of governments in many countries to alter school governance, curriculum, teaching practices, and accountability systems (OECD, 1995). For example, schools in England and Wales have been on the receiving end of a barrage of government policy shifts — local management, the removal of most of the powers of local education authorities, the need to compete for students, a national curriculum with extensive national testing and publication of results, new sets of school leaving qualifications, dramatic changes in further and higher education with important implications for secondary schools, much greater powers for school governing bodies, compulsory school inspections, and so on. In the United States and Canada change has varied considerably across states and provinces, which have jurisdiction over education, but has been enormous in many settings. The buzzword 'restructuring', while it has many meanings (Elmore, 1992), at the least implies very substantial changes in schools. Many US states have rewritten their entire education law. Among the most common initiatives have been school based management, parent councils, state testing, minimum competency requirements for graduation, takeovers of failing schools, significant changes in finance, and racial integration policies. In Canada provinces have been extending provincial achievement testing, reducing the numbers and powers of school districts, imposing new curriculum requirements, and freezing or cutting funding to schools. In several countries large-scale change models such as Success for All, the Coalition of Essential Schools, and Accelerated Schools have become increasingly influential.

All of this has occurred in a climate, in recent years, of harsh criticism of schools, limited or reduced levels of funding, and the replacement of a dynamic of hope and optimism with one of fear and frustration. Government policy documents typically take the view that school systems have failed to deliver what is required, and that the failure is especially lamentable in view of the high level of spending on education. Many other reports in many different countries by various commissions and interest groups make similar claims (Beare and Boyd, 1993). The general tone underlying much reform is negative — an effort to undo alleged damage.

Unravelling these paradoxes requires some discussion of the nature of relationships between organizations and their environments generally. Although there are insights to be obtained from the literature in these areas, some limits of conventional thinking also need to be explored before turning in later chapters to our own data and interpretations.

Understanding Organization–Environment Links

There is a consensus in the literature on schools and on organizations generally that organizations must adapt to changes in their environments if they are to survive. This is the essence of an open systems model of organizations, which remains the standard conceptualization. 'When environments change, organizations face the prospect either of not surviving or of changing their activities in response to these environmental factors' (Pfeffer and Salancik, 1978). Biological metaphors are common in this discussion; organizations are compared with species or are described as living in ecosystems. Concepts of birth and death, survival and adaptation are often invoked. The work of leaders and managers is seen to be key to the ability of organizations to survive and prosper under changing conditions.

The matter of organization response to environmental change is, however, not nearly as simple as these metaphors suggest.

For one thing, the question of what constitutes the 'environment' of an organization is not straightforward. Much of the literature treats environment as a kind of residual concept. For example, in a popular book of the 1980s, Bolman and Deal (1984) describe the environment as 'everything outside the boundaries of an organization, even though the boundaries are often nebulous and poorly drawn' (p. 44).

Support for this all-encompassing sense of environment comes from data collected from school administrators. In one study, surveys returned by ninety-two administrators identified a total of 752 different problems or issues facing the schools (Fris and Balderson, 1988). No single issue was ranked as most important by more than a quarter of the respondents, suggesting very little consensus on these matters. In another study, twenty-one principals identified a total of 907 issues or problems in sixteen different categories, although most of these concerned the internal operations of the school (Leithwood, Cousins and Smith, 1990). In effect, the environment could be understood to include anything which might affect the schools, and that potentially means everything.

That people can list issues does not mean that they agree on either their nature or importance. What one person sees as critical another may regard as largely irrelevant; what seems a threat to one is an opportunity to another; a problem located in the community by one person may be seen as residing largely within the school by someone else. The data we report in this book support earlier studies showing little consensus among educators on the nature of change, on which issues are most important, or on what should be done about them. Polling of the public also shows little agreement on the key issues facing education. Both Canadian and United States polls of 'the most significant problems facing schools' typically show no issue being rated as the number one problem by more than 15 percent of respondents, and there is little agreement even on the top five issues (Williams and Millinoff, 1990; Elam and Rose, 1995).

If everything is potentially important, and time and energy are not available to address every issue, then it is important to understand the process through which some items are given salience over others — what we describe as 'learning'. Recent years have seen the rapid growth of work around the idea of 'organizational learning' and 'the learning organization'. The idea here is to work to increase the capacity of organizations to learn about and respond to their changing situation. Peter Senge's 1990 book *The Fifth Discipline* is among the best known earlier works in this field, but the idea has caught on rapidly and there are now large popular and academic literatures on organizational learning (e.g., Argyris, 1992; Levitt and March, 1988; Simon, 1991; Watkins and Marswick, 1993).

Organizational learning is an attractive idea, but not without its problems. Much of the work is highly abstract, and doesn't deal with real organizations and the barriers they face. It tends to assume a world of rational analysis and optimizing behaviour, and one in which there is general agreement on what needs to be learned. The important question of what constitutes 'learning' in an organization is sometimes glided over. The best available evidence is that the process of learning in organizations is a very uncertain one, for three linked reasons. First, the very complexity of the world makes it unlikely that any simple or straightforward understanding of events and circumstances can be obtained, or would be useful if it could be obtained. Second, there is considerable research which illustrates the limits of human ability to process complex information. And third, our organizational forms and practices also place limits on our ability to see and to deal with changes in the world around us.

Political scientist Yehezkel Dror is particularly eloquent in regard to the first point, the complexity of a changing world. In discussing what he calls 'policy adversities', Dror notes that these are very complex, include many interacting and dynamic factors, seem to be highly intractable, may be exogenous to government, and involve inherent contradictions (1986, pp. 38–45). For example, schools are subject to pressures to reduce spending, increase services, put more stress on academic performance, keep more students in school, decentralize authority, and meet regional or even national standards. It is not just that these pressures are inconsistent, but also that they interact with each other to produce even more complex patterns of demand and response. The emerging science of chaos (Gleick, 1987) has illuminated the difficulties in studying systems which, while they display certain stabilities or patterns at the aggregate level, are almost completely unpredictable at the micro level, or vice versa. From another perspective, Peter Vaill has described the current setting for organizations as being akin to 'permanent white water' (Vaill, 1989).

Not only is the world immensely complex, but human ability to deal with complexity appears to be highly constrained. Recent literature in cognitive psychology and related fields has taught us much about the ways in which people form judgments and make decisions, and the limits on our ability to do so. Dror (1986), again, is particularly perceptive in describing the limits of human and organizational ability to understand and cope with complexity and adversity. For example, people tend to overestimate the influence of immediate or visible causal agents — the obvious instead of the important. We tend not to see the importance of subtle and long-term changes, to infer causality when events are connected only fortuitously, to give too much weight to what we have seen or been told most recently, and to be powerfully influenced by preconceptions and stereotypes (Kiesler and Sproull, 1982). Some of these patterns of sense-making will be explored further in later chapters.

How people make sense of the world also depends greatly on the organizational setting (March and Olsen, 1989). What information is widely circulated and regarded as credible? What sorts of ideas are seen as acceptable and which are not? What communication patterns exist? What has been past practice? What myths and stories shape the way people think about their organization? What language is commonly used (since what has no name is all but invisible)? All these factors will influence the way that people think about the world they inhabit.

McCall and Kaplan (1985), studying decision-makers, describe various sources from which a sense of problem or issue may emerge, including organizational routines, values, other people, and direct experience. They see the process of problem identification as interactive, and as affected by such factors as previous mental sets and emotional responses. From the very large number of problems which are thus perceived at any particular time, people select those which will be acted upon — again through processes which are not well understood. McCall and Kaplan identify influences such as receiving an instruction to do something, seeing the problem as being one's own, seeing the possibility of a solution, the history of the issue, the perceived degree of crisis involved, and the existence of deadlines. The kind of careful analysis prescribed in works on planning is not typical; in fact, priorities often get set by chance.

In an important sense, identification or understanding of issues and changes is always local. The literature on schools and change may talk in terms of macro trends — changing technology, changing patterns of work, changing modes of organizing. But what people actually see in their daily lives are local and concrete manifestations of larger trends. We may all agree that 'the global economy' is an important change affecting education, but the meaning of this phrase will be quite different in a large urban centre and in a small rural community. Consider these instances, drawn from the school districts in our study:

1   A suburban high school has seen its community and student population change over the past twenty years from white and middle-class to extremely diverse ethnically and economically. The teaching and organizational strategies that seemed successful two decades ago don't work nearly as well now, but nobody is sure what to do about it.

2   A rural school district, which at one time had half a dozen thriving towns, now really has only two communities that may have long-term viability as the rural population continues to decline and successful students move away to pursue jobs. The schools take pride in preparing young people but know that this means the continued diminution of their communities and way of life.

3   An urban school district is trying to respond to a growing and increasingly well-organized Aboriginal community demanding to know why its children have been so unsuccessful in the schools. How does the district reconcile its commitment to education for all with the particular needs and aspirations of its various sub-communities?

4   A suburban-rural district used to be a series of small towns in which everyone knew everyone, but is now largely a bedroom community with many group and foster homes and a high incidence of special needs students. Can an approach to schooling rooted in a close-knit community work under these circumstances?

5   A First Nations school authority on an Indian reservation struggles with the meaning of quality education for native people and its implications for their traditional way of life. Now that they control their own schools, what should those schools look like? How do they increase graduation rates and participation in post-secondary education without losing their sense of identity?

These local circumstances are at least in part the result of much larger and longer-term social trends, but it is the particulars that face people, not the larger trend. The maxim of 'think globally, act locally' is certainly applicable to change in education.

If 'learning' is a troublesome concept, so equally is 'responding'. A number of different explanations have been advanced as to why schools allegedly do not change. Some explanations focus on self-interest. For example, Marxists and critical theorists would assert that schools as presently constituted effectively advance class interests, and that changes are not made because ruling elites benefit from the present structure and functioning of schools (see Liston, 1988, for an extensive discussion of this literature). Much of the rhetoric of educational reform in the last decade, with its stress on academic standards and school choice, fits well within an explanatory framework of class interests (Barlow and Robertson, 1994). Another explanation which focuses on self-interest but from a very different, and currently more popular political stance is that of provider capture, in which school change is resisted by teachers and other professionals who benefit from the current system (Tyack and Tobin, 1994).

Quite a different perspective comes from analysts who look at the mismatch between proposed changes and the structure and governance of schooling. David Cohen is among the most eloquent proponents of this view. He argues that schools are highly decentralized, with the capacity to make changes distributed not only among levels of government but also within the school among administrators, teachers and students. Changes in learning require changes in people's behaviour that must largely be voluntary, so that nobody is in a position to impose change in practice even when there is agreement on changes in policy (Cohen, 1992). Changes in educational practice depend on changes in teachers' knowledge, their professional values and commitments and the social resources of teaching practice, yet these are not often the focus of reforms, which are themselves didactic in approach (Cohen, 1995, p. 15).

Moreover, in a period in which schooling is under attack from so many sources, it is hardly surprising that people inside the system see the merits of stability and of conserving what seems to them to have worked well. Embracing change in the abstract and for others is much easier than wholeheartedly accepting massive change in one's own immediate circumstances! If teachers are inclined sometimes to blame the problems of education on parents and students, or on government policies, this is not much different than governments blaming the problems of the economy on teachers and schools. All of us are inclined to want others to change so as to make our lives easier.

While the conventional view in the organization theory literature is that organizations must respond to external change, others see the dynamic as considerably more complex. Many of these arguments fall under the rubric of 'neo-institutionalism' (Crowson, Boyd and Mawhinney, 1996), in which organization functioning is shaped by characteristics of institutions and institutional systems rather than by rational analysis or self-interest. Institutional theorists also point to the importance of networks or systems of organizations, in which all organizations of a certain kind become very similar to each other because of regulations, professional practices, legal requirements, and other factors that may have nothing to do with the organizations' effectiveness or success.

> Institutionalized arrangements are reproduced because individuals often cannot even conceive of appropriate alternatives (or because they regard as unrealistic the alternatives they can imagine). Institutions do not just constrain options: they establish the very criteria by which people discover their preferences. In other words, some of the most important sunk costs are cognitive. (Powell and Dimaggio, 1991, pp. 10–11)

One version of this approach, originally developed in studying schools, is the 'logic of confidence' (Meyer and Rowan, 1977) which suggests that schools can remain substantively unchanged provided they are seen as embodying the right kinds of activities and processes, regardless of outcomes. Thus the changes in curriculum, or the addition of new programs and services serve to present the facade of response, while the heart of the instructional process remains unaltered. Testing students becomes a substitute for actually taking steps to improve learning.

Another perspective comes from work by Meyer and Zucker (1989) on what they call 'the permanently failing organization'. They argue that organizations are places in which multiple competing interests are at play, of which goal achievement is only one, and that organizations may accept a state of more or less permanent 'failure' because of the pressures from various internal and external constituencies to avoid radical change. Failure to respond is not a problem for such an organization, but a characteristic of it. Since schools, as public organizations, are fundamentally subject to competing interests, a pattern of response which stresses placating interests over achieving goals would be expected.

Other theorists have asserted that organizations are simply incapable, regardless of will, of changing rapidly enough to accommodate external changes. Organizations are seen as substantially controlled by environments which the organizations may not understand at all. Proponents of this view stress the inability of organizations to understand or anticipate change, as well as the limited ability of organizations to adjust when change requires it. Kaufman (1985) notes that '. . . organizations by and large are not capable of more than marginal changes, while the environment is so volatile that marginal changes are frequently insufficient to assure survival' (p. 131). Dror (1986) talks about the idea of 'fuzzy gambling', in which the odds are unknown and also shift over time, while the very rules of the game also change unexpectedly.

We are also drawn to accounts of organizational life that stress the importance of the mundane and the routine in shaping how organizations work. Among the most eloquent writers in this vein is James March, whose work over several decades points out that what people do every day is shaped less by grand design or careful analysis or even passion than it is by what was done yesterday and the day before. March (1984) points out that a considerable amount of routine is necessary. While we focus our attention on heroes and change agents, none of the heroism would be possible without a base of ongoing activity that is not subject to change and reanalysis at every moment.

March also notes the paradox that effective adaptation to change will inevitably lead to less effective adaptation in future (March and Olsen, 1989). As a strategy is found to be effective, people become committed to it and the organization develops it as standard practice (see also Miller, 1990). But as conditions change, the practice that was effective will become less so — what March calls the trade-off between exploration (or learning) and exploitation (or making use of what one has learned). Similarly, Kaufman points out that the idea of making an organization more flexible isn't necessarily helpful, since 'it is a paradox that maintaining flexibility can itself shut off options and impose limits on flexibility' (1985, p. 73).

The balance between stability and change has led some writers to speak about two levels of change — one in which practices or activities change and another, higher level in which the organization's sense of itself and its fundamental approach are altered. Cuban (1988) referred to these as first order and second order changes; schools, he suggested, make the former but not the latter. Argyris (1992) refers to single and double loop learning (the latter, much harder to do, involving learning about learning). However it may be very difficult to assess which practices are most helpful and effective, and organizations can go through long periods of looking for solutions without knowing when these may be found.

Conclusion

This brief foray through the literature on organizational learning about and responding to change shows that both concepts are problematic. There is nothing simple about the way that people in organizations, including schools, either learn about or try to respond to a changing world. Our capacities to understand, to learn and to respond are all limited in important ways. Yet change is occurring, and schools are faced with the problem of what to do. There is every reason to expect that external pressures on schools will continue and even intensify.

Some readers may find our analysis depressing, since it focuses on limitations to human capacity and action. We believe that change always requires a balance between idealism and realism. Without ideals we would not begin, but if we do not also look at what is really possible, we are likely to be taken in by charlatanism. We have had a great deal in education of simplistic nostrums that are touted as solutions and then fail, to the cost of many. These are not helpful; we need a better understanding both of what schools currently do and of what they might realistically do better. Such an understanding must be grounded in a thoughtful analysis of the overall situation in which schools exist — the changing social context that will shape the nature of education. Research points clearly to the limits of rationalism, but it offers no alternative to rationality as the primary human means of problem-solving. Hence the challenge of this book — to try to illustrate these processes of learning about, and responding to, a changing world as they actually occur in school systems and to suggest changes that might realistically be brought about.

Chapter 2

Collaborative Research and the Problem of Fair Portrayal

This chapter is about the dilemma of trying to do research that tries to be helpful, sympathetic and critical all at the same time. We provide a brief discussion of the research on which the book is based, and focus attention on the problem of conducting collaborative research.

To sort through our questions about school system responses to change we have been involved for the past five years in research that draws on several sources, including a wide-ranging literature review, data from three non-school organizations — a hospital, a government department and a private sector financial services company, and especially three years of work with school districts, school administrators and policy-makers in a Canadian province.

Our research program has been primarily interpretive in orientation. We wanted to learn about how people in schools see and think about the world, and this meant talking with them and observing them. Major methodological sources included Bogdan and Biklen (1982), Dexter (1970), Guba and Lincoln (1981), Miles and Huberman (1984), Stake (1988), Tesch (1990), Walford (1991) and Yin (1989). On interviewing we made use of Dexter (1970), Mishler (1986) and Seidman (1991). We accept from the outset that our research is our creation, developed from our interests and shaped by our biographies and views, and that all the interpretations which follow are our own.

We began our work with a wide-ranging review of relevant literature, drawing not only on research in education, but also in management, sociology, social psychology and public administration. We were interested in both empirical and theoretical work in various disciplines on the ways in which organizations cope with changing environments. The education literature on these issues is relatively sparse but many important insights can be found in work in other disciplines which we cite throughout the book as it is relevant to the discussion.

The primary study on which this book is based had two main components. The first involved collaborative case studies with five school districts in a Canadian province. The purpose of these studies was to look at the range of issues that people in the districts saw themselves as facing, which ones they saw as most important, their understandings of these issues, their self-reported sources of information about the issues, and the responses they reported trying to make to the issues.

19

The second strand of the study looked in more detail at three specific issues we selected — child poverty, information technology, and change in the nature of work. In addition to information on these issues from our five partner districts, we used a variety of means — primarily interviews, surveys, and conversations — of gathering information from school board members and school administrators across the province.

In effect, one part of the study looked at many issues in a few districts; the other looked at a few issues in many districts. We thought that these two approaches would, in combination, give us a good sense of the ways in which school districts understand, learn about and respond to changes in the world around them.

The Collaborative Case Studies

The proposed collaborative focus of the study meant that we couldn't simply select districts at random. Instead, we wrote to superintendents from six districts who we thought might be interested in such a project, and invited them to participate. We also chose districts that we thought were quite different from each other and which represented a cross-section of the province (which has a total of about sixty districts), with the exception of the far northern areas where the logistics of conducting the kind of study we wanted would be too difficult.

The process of negotiating participation was different in each district, a trend that would continue through all parts of the study. In one district the superintendent simply took our letter of invitation forward to the school board, which approved the district's taking part. In two districts we met or talked with the superintendent and other administrators. One of these districts eventually declined to participate, while in the other the superintendent asked for, and received, approval by the board. In three districts we attended meetings of the school board to explain our project and answer any questions about the nature of the district's participation. All of these districts agreed to take part, leaving us with five of the original six. This approval process took some time, so that we were almost finished collecting data in the first district before we really began in the last. The districts — urban, suburban, rural, suburban-rural and Aboriginal — ranged in size from 1,100 to 32,000 students. Because the province has many districts with very small enrollments, our five districts included almost 25 percent of all students in the province. We provide a brief picture of each district in Chapter 3.

Once the districts agreed to participate, we had a relatively standard approach. We began by reviewing documents that might provide an official view of external issues. In each district we went through two or three years of school board minutes, and looked at other documents such as meetings of administrator groups, annual reports to the public, planning documents, and priority or goal statement. Our selection of documents was made in consultation with our colleagues in each district. We then conducted a series of interviews in each district. We wanted to interview school board members, superintendents, and some principals. The choice of specific people to interview was discussed in each case with the district superintendent. We wanted to get some cross-section of experience and opinion, but equally felt it important to respect any sensitivities that might exist in the district; we did not want our study to become part of ongoing conflicts.

We wrote to all those suggested for interview, inviting them to participate, noting that the choice was voluntary on their part, describing the nature and purpose of our study and describing the interview procedures. These involved our tape-recording the interview and preparing from the audiotape a detailed record of the interview. These records, however, were not verbatim transcripts. We edited what was said so that the reports were in complete sentences, grammatically correct, and with duplication of content minimized. We also gave all respondents the opportunity to review and edit as desired the report of their interview, and guaranteed that we would use for the study only the version as edited.

Some argue that these procedures are violations of basic tenets of research, in that they corrupt the data — first by rewording what people said so as to be appropriate to written language, and second by allowing them to edit their remarks. We don't accept this criticism, for several reasons. There is no reason to think that people's initial comments as stated in an interview are more accurate than their reflective editing of those comments with time to think and to see them in context. Editing the interview reports actually allows both respondents and researchers to focus on what was said instead of worrying about lapses in grammar or repetition.

The main reason for allowing editing of interview reports, however, is ethical. Although we pointed out that each individual's participation was voluntary, we also understood that the politics of a district might dictate otherwise once a person had been recommended by the superintendent. We wanted people to be as candid as they could with us. One cannot develop a collaborative research relationship with people unless they have adequate assurance that what they say cannot be used, as it were, against them or their organization. Our strategy to try to alleviate any fears about how people's words might be used was to allow them to revise what appeared in print so that they were comfortable with it. That way participants could be sure that the data we used in the study from their interview would indeed reflect their considered opinion.

In fact, most respondents made very few changes in their original summaries, and these were often to clarify points that they thought had not been adequately explained in the original discussion. Four or five colleagues out of the forty-four we interviewed made large numbers of changes (one person made two sets of revisions), and even in these cases, we do not think that their changes made the final version less informative.

In total we interviewed forty-four people, including fourteen school board members, eighteen district administrators, and twelve school administrators.

Of the district administrators, thirteen were superintendents or assistant superintendents and the others held positions such as secretary treasurer, computer coordinator, and special education coordinator. Thirty-three of those we interviewed were men; eleven were women, of whom six were school board members, four were superintendents or assistant superintendents, and one was a school administrator. This gender distribution is different from the overall population in the province, where women constitute about half of school board members, a quarter of school principals but only a very small proportion of superintendents.

District by district our interviews included:

Urban district — twelve interviews, including three school board members, five district administrators and four school administrators. Eight were men and four women.

Suburban district — ten interviews, including two school board members, six district administrators and two school administrators. Eight were men.

Suburban-rural district — seven interviews; three school board members, two district administrators and two school administrators. Six were men.

Aboriginal district — seven interviews; five school board members, one district administrator and one school administrator. Four were men.

Rural district — eight interviews; two school board members, four district administrators and two school administrators. Seven were men.

Once we had a complete set of approved interview reports we wrote a case study report for each district. There were two versions of each report — a two page summary version and a longer (approximately 15,000 words, or thirty pages) version. In each report we tried to describe for people in the district what we had learned about their understandings of, and responses to, external change. We described the range of issues identified in the documents and interviews, the degree of consensus on the most important issues, the ways in which it seemed to us these issues were understood, the sources of information about external issues that had been identified, and the strategies they had told us they were using to respond to social change. We discuss the use of these reports later in this chapter. Towards the end of the research process a seminar was arranged for people from the districts (only three were able to participate), giving them an opportunity to discuss their common experiences, as well as their perspectives on the processes and outcomes of the study.

The Issues Studies

As a second element of the overall study we chose three issues to examine in more detail — child poverty, information technology, and changes in work. We selected these issues for three reasons. First, they are current and we could expect educators to have views about them. Second, all three issues have important consequences for the work of schools. Third, the issues are different in nature and likely to manifest themselves in different ways in schools. Child poverty will affect the students who come into schools, and hence the work of teaching and learning, but its effects are localized to some children and some communities. Information technology affects society broadly and is thought by many to offer potential to change teaching and learning in a direct way. Changes in work don't necessarily affect schools directly, but because preparation for work is one of the major purposes of schools, these changes may have important implications for what schools do.

We used several strategies to collect data about these issues. They were raised either by us or by our colleagues in most, but not all, of the interviews in the five partner school districts, and we use many of these conversations in later chapters. We also developed a written survey on each of the three issues and sent all three surveys to each of the sixty school board chairs and chief superintendents of schools in the province. The surveys asked about people's knowledge of the issue, their sources of information, their perspective on the importance of the issue, the strategies their district was using in regard to each issue, and their views as to the efficacy of these strategies. The formats were parallel for each issue, though the specific questions differed, of course, to reflect the issue. To try to keep response rates reasonable, the surveys were brief and required only closed-answer responses. Each survey had between forty and sixty questions. We received responses to these surveys from sixty-four people in forty-eight districts, including eighteen school board members and forty-six district administrators (in some cases the responses appear to have been delegated by the chief superintendents). Seventy percent of respondents were male, reflecting primarily the very small number of women in superintendents' positions.

Because of our interest in making our research known and useful to others in education, we also sought less formal settings to talk with people about our study and to collect data from them. We attended two regional meetings of superintendents and spent about an hour at each one talking with the superintendents (about a dozen in each case) about, in one instance, child poverty and in the other instance changes in work. We also conducted two workshops at meetings of the provincial association of school board members, attended by both school board members and board administrators. In the first of these, attended by about eighty people, we described the purpose of our study, gave participants issues to discuss in small groups, and then had a large group discussion. At the second session, a few months later, we reported some of the results of our survey and asked those attending (about sixty people) to comment on the results and to discuss their implications. Though it is difficult to report data from encounters of this kind in a standard research format, our conversations with our colleagues in these settings have influenced our thinking about the issues discussed in this book.

Doing Collaborative Research

Our intent from the beginning was to conduct research that was collaborative and useful for practice. We hoped that our research might be helpful to our colleagues and other educators in thinking through some difficult issues. We hoped that our colleagues would become full partners in the research, not just our respondents; that they would help us sort out what needed to be studied, how best to study it, and what sense to make of the results. At the same time, we wanted to avoid the frequent conceit of researchers who collect data from subjects and then use the data to point out the errors in the subjects' practice. These aspirations towards making our research a learning experience shaped the approach we took to data collection and analysis in several ways.

We recognized that this sort of approach to research is difficult to do, and is likely to have very limited impact. We have been involved in previous studies of a similar nature (Riffel and Levin, 1986; Levin, 1993) and many other researchers have also written about the difficulties of doing research that affects practice (e.g., Cooley and Bickel, 1986; Brown, 1981). Despite the obstacles, which include differing time-scales, problem-frames, ideas about evidence and relevance, and complex issues of status and power, we felt it important to try to work in a collaborative, action-oriented way.

Because of our interpretive orientation and our desire to foster dialogue, conducting the study became a considerably more challenging task. All our letters and other communications with our partner districts stressed our collaborative intention, invited our colleagues to comment on our proposals or to suggest other procedures that might be more useful or relevant to them. We wanted also to give as much information as we could back to our colleagues with the hope that they would find it useful and thought-provoking. This was another reason for asking our colleagues to read and comment on the transcripts of their interviews with us. Similarly, although the case studies of each district were written primarily to help us put their experiences into social and temporal perspective, we also hoped that the cases might spark discussion in the districts.

For the study of the three issues we also tried to build in collaborative processes. We prepared papers on issues of technology, poverty, the labour force and organizational learning, trying to analyze the way each issue was seen across all five districts. These papers, too, were circulated to people in all the districts with an invitation for comments. We offered to meet with people in the districts to discuss the issues or our study. We conducted a number of professional development sessions in which we gave participants information about our study results and talked further with them about the three issues, and we reported highlights of the survey results in several forms to school boards and superintendents. Again, we were interested in the use our colleagues might make of our research to examine and improve their own practice.

Given these strategies, our accounts of the issues, portrayal of the events and attribution of motives had to be put together in a way that would be seen by our colleagues as reasonable. We wanted the construction of cases and issue papers as well as the interpretations of their meaning to be joint processes, involving us and people from the school districts. We needed to demonstrate sensitivity to persons and their interests, something which is very hard to do when writing about people. And what we wrote or said publicly had to be politically and professionally acceptable; matters raised in the privacy of an interview do not always lend themselves to public review.

We found ourselves in an uncomfortable location, caught between the generalizations found in the academic literature and the specific practices and views mentioned by our colleagues. The role of friendly analyst was not easy to play and has not been universally accepted. For some colleagues, researchers remain experts who must have answers; for others researchers will always be irrelevant to the real problems of practice. Although we tried to present ourselves as researchers rather than as consultants, in some districts we were asked for advice or invited to comment on the state of their systems while in other districts our work was largely ignored.

We asked colleagues in all five districts to comment on whether the case study reports we constructed seemed to them an accurate portrayal of their district. One district took issue with some points in the case, and we revised it accordingly. In the others there was general acceptance that our view was a reasonable one, but certainly no wild enthusiasm for what we had said. Not surprisingly, our version of their lives didn't seem more compelling than their own understandings.

Two-column Research

In the end we don't think we were very successful in the attempt to create collaborative research. Of the five school districts, one took steps to use our case study as a vehicle for organization development. In three others we have been told that the study stimulated thinking and discussion within the organization, but have no independent means of knowing if this was so. In one district our work disappeared amidst serious internal conflicts that were preoccupying people. Several reasons can be suggested as to why this was so. It may be that we needed to invest more time and energy in building the kinds of collaborative relationships we wanted. Perhaps our initial reports and feedback to the districts were either too controversial or in other cases insufficiently interesting to retain their real collaboration. As we note elsewhere, as this study was being done schools were under considerable pressure from many sides; they may have felt that active participation in a research study was simply too low a priority to receive much time or energy. In one district almost all the senior staff left in a short time after our initial report; the tensions behind some of those departures also affected the response to our study.

Most importantly, we think, effective and meaningful research partnerships are not a common part of school practice, and a single study won't change that pattern. New ways of relating take time and effort to learn, and the interests of researchers and practitioners, as noted, are not necessarily mutually consistent. Standard ideas of what research is and how it can be done continue to exert a powerful influence.

The problems can be illustrated by excerpts from a meeting that took place with half a dozen respondents in one of the participating districts. We had sent them copies of our draft case study, and were meeting with them to get their responses. Here is a segment of our conversation:

Administrator 1: I'd like to say again that the story is useful and every quotation offers us insight into the perspective of an individual in the District. I'm just pointing out that the language you use to introduce the individual quotations gives the impression that the quotation is more than an individual perspective.

Researcher 1: Is your concern that our language implies criticisms of the District that are inappropriate?

Administrator 2: No.

Researcher 1: Then why is it an issue? I don't understand why our leads matter. If you think they are misleading, then that is certainly an important concern. However, if you do not believe they are misleading, I don't see what difference our leads make. The point is true in the abstract, but in the concrete, so what?

Administrator 2: Don't they structure what you selected from the interviews?

Researcher 1: No. It was the other way around. The quotes structured the leads. We started with the interview data, and looked at the issues, and took everything people said and looked for common themes. I think we'd argue that this is our inductive view from what you told us.

Administrator 3: So this is your perception of our perception.

Researcher 1: Yes.

Administrator 1: Even though it was the perception of a single individual, expressed by a single individual, and not expressed by the other nine.

Researcher 2: Yes, frequently that is true.

Administrator 1: You are presenting a story that appears to the reader to have a veracity to it that goes beyond an individual's perspective.

School board 1: I guess it's possible that one individual could tell a very accurate story about [our district] in a changing world. It's possible that if you took that story to a variety of individuals they could say 'yes, I think that person told an accurate story'. It's also possible that in doing it this way that you get an

> understanding that there isn't a similarity in the
> stories that you tell. Ten people tell ten different
> stories which have some similarities in some areas,
> and greater diversity in other areas. That might
> be useful as long as we keep it in that context.

The discussion continued in this vein for some time, leading one of the researchers to note:

Researcher 2: It just struck me as we've been talking about this that when we put this together we paid very little attention to our words, and were anxious to get down yours. And you've done just the . . . same. You've paid very little attention to your words, and you've focused on ours.

While we wanted to develop a collaborative description of the district's activities, our colleagues wanted a report that reaffirmed what they were doing or pointed to specific improvements they should make. It also seemed difficult to move from the individual interviews to a composite portrait of the organization. The less commonality in views within a district, the more difficult it was to construct a picture that our colleagues could recognize and accept.

We are not confident, despite our efforts, that we have managed to write about our study in a way that does truly combine critical analysis with real understanding of the challenges our colleagues face. As the dialogue illustrates, an inevitable problem is that any research of this kind transforms the words and ideas of respondents into the images of the researchers. Whatever we may do to try to represent lived experience to readers, we cannot in this book do much to convey the fullness of the ways in which our more than forty colleagues thought and spoke about these issues. Readers and our colleagues may well find that this book embodies the sort of seemingly-superior commentary that we set out to avoid. A reader with a different perspective — for example one of the hard-working and stressed administrators we interviewed — might restate our views in quite different terms:

Our perceptions	**Our colleagues' perceptions**
• importance of data	• importance of experience
• concern for analysis	• concern for acceptability
• organizations are drifting	• doing best they can under great pressure
• need for change	• tremendous constraints on change; need for stability
• politics as initiating	• politics as responding to others
• no centre or focus to activity	• big picture is impossible to get
• need for leadership	• demands come from outside
• need for pluralism	• need for control and equality of treatment

If one looks at these lists, it isn't evident that our colleagues' views are any less reasonable than those we will argue. We take the position that schools are facing great pressures to change and that the task of school leaders should be in large part to help the organization understand and respond to these changes. We believe that schools can do a better job of this than is currently being done. We understand how difficult this task can be when one is in the midst of the alligators. But some of our colleagues would not agree that what we propose is a legitimate or desirable role for them to play.

The result of this exercise is a conflicted book. We do proceed to criticize many school practices, and to suggest ways in which these could be improved. We believe that many of our proposals are both feasible and worthwhile. But we want to put this agenda forward in a way that does not demean or belittle the intentions, skills and commitment of our colleagues in education. We are not suggesting that we have the answers and they do not. We were not evaluating our colleagues or their organizations, but were trying to use our examination of these districts to make more general comments about schools and external change; comments that people in those settings might find useful. Our colleagues in these districts are indeed trying hard to do what they think is right, often under quite difficult circumstances. Of course we think some of them more talented and capable than others, but that is beside the point. Organizations always contain a mix of people, and all of these districts include many sincere, hard-working people who care deeply about education. Our intention is always to be helpful to them, not to diminish their efforts. We will remind readers of this stance at several points in later chapters.

Warrant, Use of Evidence and Quotations

Anyone writing about the results of research faces the problem of establishing the validity of findings. What makes a research finding credible? One of our colleagues, in reading an earlier version of the book, was concerned that we had used data selectively to support ideas that we had in mind before we did the research. He felt that the selective use of quotations in the book did not establish sufficient warrant for our conclusions.

Our view is that the results of social science research are never warranted strictly and only by the data. Views of social phenomena arise from the whole of one's experience, just as the questions to be asked and data to be gathered in any study are shaped by the researchers' ideas and understandings. Being able to give ten illustrative quotations to a point, rather than one or two, would not, in our minds, have made our conclusions any more 'scientific' (though it would have caused considerable grief to our publisher and taken us well over our contractual page limit for this book!). We do not, however, believe that this makes all research entirely subjective or that one finding is as good as another. We cannot here review the enormous literature on this subject — whose authors do not agree by any means on the criteria for judging the value of social science — or enter into complex questions of epistemology. We encourage each reader to regard our comments sceptically, as we try to do ourselves, and to ask if what we say seems believable, accords with the reader's own experience, and offers ways of thinking that seem to be interesting and useful.

We do make extensive use throughout the book of quotations from our interviews in the five partner school districts. We made a deliberate effort to include views from all of the districts, and from people in various capacities (district administrators, board members, school administrators) in each district. This was not always possible because the nature of the interviews varied. We interviewed more people in the larger districts, so have more data to work with. People varied in their talkativeness and their level of insight; some interviews gave us many comments we wanted to include; others very few. Our interview data are thinnest in the Aboriginal district; we did the fewest interviews there (six), and people were least inclined to be talkative with us.

The open nature of the interviews also meant that not all issues were raised in each interview. For example, many respondents talked about issues of poverty or technology, but some did not. Sometimes we deliberately raised these issues in the interview if our colleagues did not mention them, but whether this was feasible depended on many aspects of the overall interview, such as timing, flow, and mood. We acknowledge that what appears in this book is our selection of evidence consistent with the overall argument that we have developed from our work with the data. In the end the persuasiveness of our account will rest on the degree to which readers find it coherent and explanatory, rather than on some narrow compliance with a particular set of research procedures.

We use the quotations from the interviews in various ways. Many of them are relatively brief so that we can present a cross-section of comments. In some cases, however, we have included quite long excerpts from the interviews where we feel that the longer dialogue is necessary to illustrate a particular point or approach to an issue. Each quotation is identified by the district (urban, suburban, suburban-rural, rural and Aboriginal) and by the speaker's role in the district. To protect the identity of individuals, we use only three role descriptions — district administrator (superintendent, assistant superintendent, consultant, or other person working in the district office); school administrator (all principals); and school board members. Where comments in the quotations appear in **boldface** they indicate words of the interviewer.

Chapter 3

School Systems and the Changes They Face

This chapter is concerned with the kinds of external changes and pressures our colleagues in the districts see themselves as facing. Which pressures do educators and policy-makers see as most important, and why? Before turning to these questions, however, we provide some context for the study by describing the provincial setting and each of our five partner school districts.

The Provincial Context

Our study was set in a smaller Canadian province much of whose population live in the capital city or in the southern part of the province in small cities and towns. Most of the province's territory is empty; the north, which accounts for two-thirds of the area, has about 5 percent of the population. The province used to be primarily agricultural, and agriculture remains a strong part of the culture although it now accounts for only a small fraction of the provincial economy, which is highly diversified including mining, lumbering, both heavy and light industry and a wide array of services. For most of the last fifty years the province has exported people, especially educated young people, who move to other parts of Canada where there are greater economic opportunities. The province was settled by Europeans and organized as a province more than a century ago, and now has a considerable stability of population and outlook. There is a strong streak of individualism and self-reliance, particularly in rural parts of the province, but also a strong labor movement and a long history of co-operative organizations. The provincial government has alternated for many years between conservative and mildly left-wing parties.

Like many parts of North America, schooling in this province began largely as efforts by local settlers, sometimes organized by churches, to create schools. The urbanization following World War II was coupled with a reduction from more than 2,000 school districts (mostly with one school) to the present 60 or so districts. School enrollments peaked in 1971, fell by about 25 percent over the next fifteen years, and have been roughly stable since then. However there has been continued population movement from rural to urban areas, so that many rural districts now enroll fewer than 1,500 students.

Legislative authority over education in Canada rests with provincial governments. The Minister of Education, a member of the Cabinet, is highly important, but key policy decisions will be made by the government as a whole. The provincial Department of Education, headed by a Deputy Minister, is responsible for policy implementation on behalf of the government. However all provinces have delegated many management functions to local school districts. School districts are governed by elected school boards with from five to fourteen members. Districts normally employ a superintendent as chief administrator, and depending on size may employ a few or many other central board office staff. Given the geographic make-up of the province, urban districts tend to be relatively large in population and small in area, and rural districts are the reverse. The province also contains a number of small and very remote settlements that have one school in the district, though these played little or no role in our study.

Over the years the role of the provincial Department of Education has changed substantially. At one time the Department regulated the curriculum in detail, ran examinations for students at all levels, and employed inspectors to check on whether teachers were following prescribed practices. Beginning twenty-five or thirty years ago, school districts were given much more autonomy in regard to curriculum. Provincial examinations disappeared, as did provincial inspectors. Teachers had more scope to pursue their own interests and styles. Districts, in response, added staff such as consultants to provide assistance — or sometimes direction — to teachers and schools. The Department tried to work collaboratively with school districts in important areas of policy.

At the time of our study, these patterns were changing, creating a lot of turmoil in the school systems of the province. Part of the change was financial; provincial government funding to districts for education had not kept up with inflation for a number of years. The province and school boards had coped with their financial difficulties by reducing programs such as special education and counselling and by requiring teachers and administrators to accept wage freezes or reductions. All of the districts cut back the number of teaching and administrative positions, and the province's Department of Education was dramatically downsized.

At the same time, the practice of developing education policy through processes involving extensive consultation with the major organizations has been changing. Within a few months of taking office in 1993, a new Minister of Education announced a series of important changes to various aspects of educational policy. He linked these quite openly to his belief that schools were not performing well and that the educational establishment — teachers, administrators and school boards — were largely responsible for the problems. The new proposals included the reintroduction of province-wide examinations at several grade levels, the requirement for numerical marks to replace anecdotal reporting, changes in curriculum based on a universal set of provincially defined outcomes, a program of parent choice of schools, and the creation of compulsory school level advisory councils on education from which teachers were largely excluded. The province also commissioned a review of school district boundaries, the object apparently being a significant reduction in the number of school boards, elected school trustees and their administrative staffs. Needless to say, these actions were controversial with teachers, administrators and school board members.

The Five School Districts

While the provincial context of controversy and uncertainty about educational policy had an effect on our study, our main interest was in the five school districts who were our partners in the research.

In the next few pages we provide a brief description of each of the districts. Although the districts were not selected to be representative, as a group they vary quite markedly in size, setting, population and political dynamics.

The Rural District

A drive through the rural school district would reveal large tracts of farm land, mostly growing grain. The farms appear prosperous — buildings are by and large well kept and modern, and one will see a great deal of expensive machinery in the fields during growing season. The terrain is largely flat, and there are few houses to be seen in most areas. Occasionally one comes across a village, and there are two larger towns that have a certain amount of bustle, with pick-up trucks lining the main business street. Agriculture is clearly dominant here, and the pace of life is different than in urban areas. Many people have lived in the district all their lives, so friendships and social relations tend to be long-standing.

The district enrolls approximately 1,300 students in eight schools serving an area that covers roughly 1,000 square kilometres several hours drive from a large city. There are fewer and fewer farmers, and more and more of the population, which in the aggregate has been declining steadily for many years, lives in the main towns of the districts, while some of the smaller communities have virtually disappeared. The population is relatively homogeneous — largely British background with a significant subpopulation from one particular religious group. One feature noted by several people we interviewed is the growth in group homes and foster homes, resulting in a significant increase in students entering the schools with special needs.

The school board consists of nine members, elected from three wards or areas within the district. The board meets twice a month and has a number of committees that also meet regularly. As with most school boards, for the most part the work of the board attracts little public attention unless a particular controversy arises. Also like many rural districts, the central office staff is very small — a superintendent, a special education coordinator, a computer consultant (a position that was disappearing at the time of our study), a secretary-treasurer and some office staff. The superintendent was hired from outside the district several years ago. Principals of schools operate with considerable autonomy. The district has about 100 teachers, 230 total staff, and a budget of a little less than 8 million dollars per year.

For several years the district encountered serious financial and political problems, resulting in some bitter conflict among communities who felt that their town was being treated unfairly when budget cuts were made. Over the last decade student enrollment has declined from about 1,600 to about 1,300. But there is now a widely shared feeling among those with whom we spoke that the district has left this very difficult period behind and is well positioned for continuing development. The general population decline has slowed and in some communities school enrollments have begun to grow slowly. The overall economy of the district is more robust than a decade ago, and one of its centers is experiencing a small economic boom. People are more optimistic, less preoccupied with their own economic survival. The school district itself has moved from a serious budget deficit to a modest surplus, the politics of the district are gentler, cutbacks are seen as things of the past, the morale of the staff is high, the district has begun hiring new teachers again, and it has made a significant commitment to educational technology. Parents and the communities at large are very supportive of education, and this is seen as an important asset to the school board as well as to school administrators and teachers.

The Urban District

Travelling through the urban district involves stark contrasts. In parts one finds quiet streets with large older homes on tree-filled lots. The commercial streets have exclusive clothing stores, upscale restaurants and specialized food merchants. As one moves across the district one passes through the central business area of the city with its main office buildings and department stores, and then through a series of increasingly poor residential areas. Houses and lots get smaller and more of them are poorly maintained. Local stores are now often pawn shops, used goods, and cafes. One area is very much a skid row, with mission houses, a large number of beer halls, and boarded up commercial buildings. As one moves from richer to poorer areas, the population includes more and more non-white faces. The main office of the school district is located at one end of the district, on the edge of a large commercial and industrial area, but also near a district of modest homes that were originally built for railway workers.

The urban district enrolls more than 30,000 students in eighty schools. It employs more than 2,700 teachers, a total staff of almost 4,000, and has an annual budget of more than $200 million. The board consists of nine elected trustees, three from each of three wards. The wards are very large — as many as 70,000 voters in each — so trustees can have only very limited contact, no matter how hard they work, with most electors and parents. The district has a large (though diminishing) central office, including five superintendents, several other directors and supervisors, and staff for such other functions as finance, computer services, and curriculum consultants. The chief superintendent has held his position for well over a decade. Enrollment, following the provincial pattern, has remained roughly stable over the past decade.

In addition to size, the urban district has several other distinctive features. It takes in the entire central part of the capital city, including the core area and the central business district, thus having the largest concentration both of economic activity and of poverty in the province. While much of the district is either poor or working class, it also has significant middle class and wealthy areas. The district's schools include some of the poorest and richest areas in Canada. The students are very diverse, with a large and growing Aboriginal population (estimated at 20 percent of the overall enrollment) and many immigrants from all parts of the world. As has been the case for Canada as a whole, recent immigrants have come largely from Asia and Latin America rather than from Europe. At one time the district's boundaries were coterminous with those of the city, but twenty-five years ago the city boundaries changed, and now the population of the district is no longer held together by very much common sense of identity at all.

Educational politics in the urban district have tended to be more overt and more openly conflictual than in most other jurisdictions, although the severe conflicts one might expect between, say, wealthy and poor areas have not been very evident. The district has gradually developed and organized processes that encourage more open political activity than is the norm in school systems. Elections are contested by political parties, unlike most districts in the province. Over the years the school board has quite often been split 5–4 on political lines.

Because of its size and unique composition, the district tends to see itself as quite distinct from all other districts in the province. It has also been prepared to challenge the provincial government politically over issues such as funding.

The Suburban-rural District

One reaches the suburban-rural district office by driving about three-quarters of an hour from the capital city. Almost the entire area is now built up with housing, although there is still some farmland along the route. Over the years the highways into this district have been steadily improved partly because it is on the route to some of the main vacation areas in the province. One encounters prosperity — new houses and developments, some of them quite exclusive — mixed with old and seemingly run-down farms and some older and very modest housing. If one drives farther away from the city, the terrain is very sparsely populated, with large tracts entirely empty.

The district takes in a large area, about 100 miles from north to south, and about thirty miles from east to west. Its population is about 60,000, most of whom live in the part of the district close to the provincial capital. The district could be described as largely ex-urban, with many people who make their living in or near the capital. However the main town (population 10,000) has a local economy and history of its own, and another area is centered around the resource and tourist economies of a large lake. Socio-economically the area is mixed, but generally far from wealthy. The district also enrolls some students from an Aboriginal community.

The district's thirteen schools enroll about 4,700 students, down over 10 percent during the last decade or so. One key aspect of the district is that it has a single high school. The district employs more than 300 teachers, 500 total staff, and has an annual budget of well over 20 million dollars. The board consists of ten trustees, elected from six wards. The central office staff is small — a superintendent (new to the district and the position as our study began), an assistant superintendent, a secretary-treasurer, a special education coordinator, and some support staff.

People in the district are well aware of the important role the district's geography plays in its development and operation. On one hand, they see their communities as relatively small, close-knit, and avoiding the anxieties of urban life. Yet they also see the communities becoming more influenced by the city as the number of commuter residents grows. As population shifts, the district is becoming more diverse. As in the rural district, suburban-rural district faces growth in group homes and foster homes with students with special needs.

The politics of education have never been very prominent in this district. People can get quite riled about such matters as transportation routes, but the district has been able to avoid serious conflict and divisiveness.

The Aboriginal District[1]

The Aboriginal school district serves a community of some 2,600 people on an Indian reserve, also called a First Nations community. The reserve was created a hundred years ago by a treaty between the First Nation and the Government of Canada. One reaches the reserve after several hours drive from the capital city. The roads are good until one actually enters the reserve property, where they are gravel and prone to be very muddy or very dusty. The community's housing is scattered widely across the reserve, although there is some concentration in the center of facilities such as the school, Band office, health center, recreation hall, and a couple of cafes. One sees very little commercial activity; many services are only available in the towns a few miles off the reserve. The housing is generally small and of poor quality. The concentration of young people is also noticeable, and of course the entire population is Aboriginal. At the end of the main road from the highway is a large lake, and part of the reserve land is also used for farming and ranching, as is the case for the population outside the boundaries of the reserve.

The school enrolls about 1,100 students, with 1,500 projected within ten years. Population growth has been so rapid that the nearly-new school is regarded as seriously overcrowded and the primary grades have been moved to a different building. All students are Aboriginal.

The school is governed by what is called an Educational Foundation, but which operates very similarly to a school board. Six members are elected at large in the community. (In some First Nations communities the school board is appointed by the Chief.) The Educational Foundation employs an administrator — much like a superintendent — and appropriate support staff. The school has a principal and two vice-principals, about sixty-five teachers, and 135 total staff. The total budget for the school is about 6 million dollars annually.

The central story of education in the community is the story of the community's takeover of education from the federal government about twenty years ago and its efforts since then to develop schools that truly serve the needs of the community and its people. For most of the history of the reserve, schooling was provided by the federal government, often through the agency of religious bodies, and was primarily intended to assimilate native people to European culture. Many people in the community remember going to the local residential school, where they could not see their parents — who lived in the same community — except on weekends, and where their language, traditions and values, and sometimes the students themselves were at best ignored and at worst attacked. Not surprisingly, failure and dropout rates were very high in this system (Barman and McCaskill, 1986; Haig-Brown, 1988). For many years education was a vehicle of colonization rather than helpful to the lives of reserve residents. That bitterness still lingers.

Education here also needs to be seen in the context of life in a reserve community, a relatively small and homogeneous place in which people all know each other and many are related. In contrast to this close social fabric, Aboriginal communities are also characterized by high levels of poverty, low levels of education in the adult population, and poor infrastructure (such as housing, roads, and public services). Lacking a tax base, they are largely dependent on budgets provided by the federal government. A large proportion of the population is supported by social assistance, although there has been an increase in recent years in farming, ranching, and small business in the community.

The community faces the formidable challenge of maintaining and, perhaps, redefining, an Aboriginal culture and way of life in the present times. Aboriginal people, in this community and elsewhere, are by no means agreed on what form their lives should take, what role their traditional culture and language should play, and how they should position themselves in regard to the larger society. New forms of governance, of education, and of economic activity are all emerging. Given these struggles, very little about education can be taken for granted here, yet there is an abiding sense of optimism.

The Suburban District

Travelling through the suburban district provides fewer contrasts than in some of the other settings. As in suburban areas in many cities one moves from modest homes in the older areas, which originally served a working-class population, to some very large and expensive homes in the newer parts of the district. Streets are peaceful, houses generally well kept, there are many small apartment blocks, some busy commercial areas and, at the far end of the district, some agricultural land.

For much of the last twenty years, growth has been a prominent feature of the district. Its enrollment increased from 8,500 students to 10,000 students, and several new schools were added over the past decade, making twenty-two in total. The district employs more than 700 teachers, about 1,500 total staff, and has a budget of more than 50 million dollars per year. (During the course of our study, the district lost a school and about 500 students through transfer to a newly created Francophone school district.) Though growth has tended to soften some of the financial pressures that other districts have experienced, it has brought its own problems. Socio-economic differences between parts of the district are becoming noticeable as the older part of the district becomes poorer. Some of the growth has been due to immigration, resulting in a much more diverse population which in turn led to new programs, a strain on student services, and the need for more multicultural awareness. It does seem that what was once a small closely knit community in a geographic enclave of the city is becoming more cosmopolitan. Growth probably has contributed to political changes in the district as well as to a growing formality in the district's operating procedures. Public expectations of the district's schools are high and increasingly broad, and many parents are quite demanding.

The district has a board of seven trustees, all elected at large. Its central administration at the time our study began consisted of a superintendent (who had been there a few years, hired from outside the district), three assistant superintendents, a secretary treasurer, some consultants, and various support staff — roughly typical of urban school districts of similar size.

To an outside observer the district's situation appears similar to that of other urban districts, yet it has had a high level of political controversy. A superintendent was fired a few years ago, and most of the school trustees were defeated in one recent election because of controversy over various policies, including language — long a lightning rod in Canadian education politics. A considerable amount of conflict appears to relate to the efforts of the board and central administration to have a more standardized, policy-driven approach rather than allowing as much leeway as in past to individual schools.

The Range of Issues

Having provided some information about the districts, we turn next to the issues that were identified in each setting as most important.

Our first attempt to learn about the external issues each district saw as important was through reviewing school board and administrative agendas, minutes, plans, annual reports and other documents. These documents did not prove very helpful; we found few mentions of external issues in the documents we reviewed in any of the districts. The vast bulk of issues considered by school boards and administrative groups concerned the internal operations of the organization, whether administrative or programmatic. The documents had quite a bit to say about finances, personnel, program, and the like, but little about such matters as changes in families, the implications of technology, or the other sorts of long-term issues which were of primary interest to us. None of the districts had a regular place on the agenda or process for reviewing external change and its impact on them. None of the districts had a formal strategic plan or statement of what the district saw as its long term objectives and strategies, although districts had developed mission statements, principles of teaching and learning, annual priority statements and other similar policies.

The absence of external issues from formal documents does not mean that they were never discussed. One person suggested that discussions of these larger issues tend to occur informally and off the record, and so would not be found in official documents. And few of our colleagues in our interviews seemed to give much importance to formal documents as sources of information or direction. Nonetheless, simply by reading the formal documents one would not gain any sense of social, economic or political changes as having an important place in the work of these districts. We have more to say about this issue in later chapters.

The interviews, as we expected, provided a much better sense of how people in each district saw external changes and issues affecting them. The districts differed considerably in the range of issues raised in the interviews. Table 3.1 lists the issues identified by significant numbers of our colleagues in each district. Several factors made the task of trying to assemble coherent pictures of responses to social change — first in each district and then for all of them collectively — difficult and in some cases controversial. As the table indicates, the range of issues and social changes confronting the districts was wide. Nor is this list exhaustive; we have worked with many groups of educators who easily and quickly identify thirty or forty external pressures that they consider important. As noted in Chapter 1, other studies of educators have also found long lists of issues, with relatively little consensus among them.

Some of the issues mentioned most often, such as budget pressures, were not surprising. Money is the oil of any organization, and shortages of it make the lives of administrators and policy makers more difficult and more conflictual. But there were other issues that we thought would arise, such as growing and

Table 3.1: Issues identified in interviews by district

Urban District (12 interviews)	Suburban District (10 interviews)	Suburban-rural District (7 interviews)	Rural District (8 interviews)	Aboriginal District (7 interviews)
Aboriginal education (6)	shortage of money (8)	financial pressures (7)	drugs and alcohol (4)	preparation for work (5)
changing economy (5)	technology (7)	technology (7)	local economy (3)	decreasing dropouts (3)
provincial funding (5)	purpose of schools/ public expectations (5)	dysfunctional families/ parenting (7)	increasing expectations of schools (3)	parent involvement (3)
public dissatisfaction with schools (4)	growth of ethnic/ ESL population (4)	violence/behaviour (7)		
changing parent role (4)	dysfunctional families (4)	transportation (7)		
board role and politics (4)	violence/discipline (4)	special needs students (66)		
changes in families (4)	poverty (4)	student health issues (5)		
race, ethnicity, diversity (4)	employment opportunities (4)	employment opportunities (5)		
violence in schools (4)	nature of teaching staff (4)	inter-divisional cooperation (4)		

diversifying public expectations, changes in employment patterns, or the demands of economic change. To be sure, some of our colleagues did speak
about these issues, but none of them was mentioned by even a majority of
those we interviewed. And some issues were hardly mentioned at all. Concerns about the environment and sustainable development — a major topic of
provincial policy — were hardly ever mentioned by our colleagues. As another
example, although many people spoke about changes in families and values,
only a very few mentioned changes in gender roles although this must surely
be one of the most important social changes of this century.

We also note from these lists that for those working in the field, issues
arrive in a jumble, all crowded together, and few of our colleagues appear to
have, or at least spoke to us in terms of a map that would help them sort out
in their own minds differences among the issues facing them. Our colleagues'
emphasis was clearly on those issues that were immediately present in their
work lives, the issues that walked in the door or landed on the desk. Anything
more distant or less direct tended to receive less mention. They may lack the
time for this sort of mapping — after all, the daily pressures on many of our
colleagues are intense — or they may not see the value of organizing issues
as a way of trying to manage them. As will be discussed later, the structure of
work in these districts also does not encourage or support efforts to think

about issues more analytically. However we heard much less about longer-term and large-scale issues than we did about more immediate pressures. The language of 'internal' and 'external' issues — those arising from inside the organization versus those pressing upon the system from outside — is not the way in which most of our colleagues think about change.

Another way of putting the situation is that for most of our colleagues, their everyday work in schools formed the frame of their understanding, and external social change was seen against this backdrop. In other words, changes outside the school mattered insofar as they affected what happened in the school. For us as researchers, the situation is reversed. It is social change that forms the frame against which the work of schools should be seen, and what happens in the school is judged in part on the extent to which it fits with the larger social context.

Part of the pattern of responses from our colleagues may have been due to the nature of our research. In the letter we sent to each of our colleagues before their interview we noted that we hoped to get a sense of the external issues they thought were most important. We said nothing about short- and long-term issues either in the letter or in the interviews themselves. Given their generally hectic schedules, many people did little or no preparation for the interview (nor did we ask them to prepare). It is therefore not surprising that we heard about what was on people's minds at the moment, and it is quite likely that our colleagues do have views on many longer-term issues even where these did not emerge in the interviews.

Perhaps most striking is the lack of consensus within most districts on key issues. We expected that people who worked together relatively closely, as many of our colleagues in each district did, would share a common understanding of the main pressures facing them. Yet in only one district — the suburban-rural — did our colleagues express a high degree of consensus in their listing of key external issues. In the other four districts we found much less consensus on these forces. In some districts there was little overlap in the issues identified by different respondents. Consensus might especially be expected in smaller, more homogeneous districts where the people we interviewed talked with each other more frequently and lived in similar settings. In the Aboriginal district, for example, everyone lived and worked in the same community, and most had done so for most of their lives. Smaller communities might also contain greater pressure for conformity, so that people feel more constrained to 'toe the party line'. On the other hand, in urban settings the staff may well live far from the neighborhoods in which they work and may have little to do with other colleagues outside of work. And the districts themselves are larger and less homogeneous. The urban district, particularly, embodies so much diversity that a school principal working in an affluent part of the district would face a very different world from those working in the inner-city. Yet our colleagues in the small rural district seemed no more agreed on the changes facing them than did their urban or suburban counterparts.

That people mentioned the same issue does not mean that they agreed on its nature or significance. Consider these two comments, on the matter of the importance of information technology, from people working in the same office in the same district.

Recently, what we are seeing emerging is the electronic highway or Internet, and all of a sudden, from a professional point of view, when we think that while we have been moving towards being research-based in our actions, now every school will be able to do an ERIC search. That to me is significant in itself. There is a danger, however, that we may just stay at the surface and that we are amazed by the sheer amount of knowledge, but never go in depth. This will lead to our goals being too general. That is one of the dangers we have to look at. We have to go beyond the novelty of accessibility of information and really explore how we can use the information. And, more importantly, ask: 'What information am I looking at before I even go into it, to become more efficient.' (Suburban district administrator)

I see technology as an unproven bandwagon that demands dollars but has not demonstrated its contribution to student learning. There is public pressure to go the technology route in the sense that they feel that the kids need to become technologically literate in order that they have the skills necessary to be competitive in the workforce. Some people tell me that we need to give kids twelve years of technology. I ask why? In spite of all this talk about technology I think that only a small percent of jobs require moderate levels of skill in technology. (Suburban district administrator)

Or these two rural respondents talking about drugs and alcohol.

I think alcohol is a big problem in the schools in [this district] and that it has a real effect on the kids.
. . . The acceptance by most of society, and I think the relief by many parents that even though the kid is drinking, at least he's not using drugs. Of course alcohol is the most damaging drug there is. There is an increased use of soft drugs in the area too. I think society accepts that this is ok. I know that one mom buys her 16-year-old son alcohol and cigarettes when he wants them because she thinks if she doesn't, someone else will. (Rural district school administrator)

Question So that the things that are the preoccupations of urban school administrations, violence, drugs, alcohol, abuse, those are not major things here?
They are not major, however the problem still exists here. Our principals and our administration know that there is a zero tolerance level and they have the right to put a stop to that as quickly as they can. (Rural district school board member)

Question And you're able to get the community behind you on that in a way that might be harder in an urban environment.
Definitely. Our community, being much smaller, most people know everybody in the community, so it's quite close. (Rural school board member)

Differences were also apparent on other issues. For example, some colleagues saw financial restraint as prohibiting innovation, while others felt restraint led to innovation. Some saw parents as increasingly interested in their children's education — indeed, sometime too demanding — while others felt that many parents either lacked time or interest for education. We will explore some of these differences more fully in later chapters; at this point we only want to note the very considerable differences of opinion as to what issues were important and what the significance of any given issue might be.

We are not implying that differences over issues are necessarily a problem. Consensus on key issues should not always be desperately sought. Much is written in current literature about the need for a common vision. Indeed this is one of the key factors identified in the literature on effective schools and on educational leadership (e.g., Leithwood, 1992). Organizations do need enough agreement on critical challenges to enable them to act effectively. But too much uniformity of view is as problematic as too little, since it stifles the new ideas that organizations also need and can lead to a narrow and superficial view (March and Olsen, 1989; Lindblom, 1990). The key issue is not so much the amount of agreement within an organization, as whether the organization has systematic ways of raising and discussing issues so as to determine the implications of issues and develop strategies for coping with them.

Overall Attitudes to Social Change

Nearly all of our colleagues saw the pressures of social change increasing and becoming more diverse and intense. They also saw social change as making their work more difficult.

When I first started, there was no question in my mind that I could 'handle' almost any child. Twelve years ago was the first time I met a 5-year old I couldn't handle. That's not unusual today — there's a growing number of children who have problems and are extremely hard to manage and work with. (Suburban district administrator)

Some of our colleagues appeared to resent many of the social changes they observed. They believed that many changes were for the worse, and moving along a course that could not be corrected. For these individuals, change was having debilitating social, educational and personal effects.

Question Is there trouble on the horizon?
There likely is, but hopefully I won't be here.

Question I am trying to get a sense of how you see the district. Would language like the following be helpful in describing the district? Generally prosperous, generally stable, generally quite traditional in the good sense of that term, but with a small and perhaps growing dark side which is exemplified in abuse and the excessive use of alcohol, inappropriate behavior on the part of kids, disrespect for themselves and those in positions of authority? Do you have some fear that the dark side will grow?
That is accurate. There is no doubt that the dark side likely will grow. I do not see anything out there that is going to halt it at all.

Question What would be the reason for the growth of that?
I really do not know. It may be because people do not really care. (Rural district administrator)

A similar number saw social change as an ally — a reason and an opportunity to change education in ways they valued but couldn't accomplish without external support and justification.

The focus of the school is to celebrate diversity rather than to celebrate homogeneity. We need to get kids ready to go into a very uncertain world. We can probably do that best by keeping their minds open to receive a whole number of ideas and to be problem solvers. If you want your kids to do that, you have to expect that your teachers will problem solve in the same way. So, yes, part of it is the kind of staff we went out to hire, and also the people who were already here. Diversity of teaching staff and openness to look at new ideas is a definite factor. (Suburban district school administrator)

I've seen such a difference with the ability of the system to look at a more community based decision making. We have all the advisory committees. Each school is fed into a larger structure that makes recommendations to the board. There's more discussion on meaningful stuff at my level. We are seeing much more systemic change because superintendents are sitting down with communities. (Urban district school board member)

Most of our colleagues tended toward ambivalence, being prepared to accept social change and to acknowledge the need for an educational response, but unclear whether they had the skill, time, resources and political support to cope with its demands.

From my perspective, change has had both a positive and negative impact. It is positive in the sense that its making the administration reassess many of the things we do. Sometimes in that reassessment we need to question the value of what we do, and, on occasion, discard or change things or approaches.

On the negative side, the change in the availability of funds has forced us to learn to think differently, and it is difficult for us to change our way of thinking with respect to new initiatives. Until we learn to think of innovative approaches within a milieu of restraint, the change is negative because it limits the system and it limits the way we think about ourselves. From an abstract point of view, I don't think the limitation is a necessary one. I do find, however, that it is sometimes difficult to persuade people to change, and to discard old ways of approaching things.

This change also has a negative impact on personnel. Some people are reluctant to change the way that they think about educational resources because it will force them to change their personal frames of reference; other people perceive changes in approach or in the organization as devaluing their work. (Suburban district administrator)

For people inclined to ambivalence, social change was often experienced as an educational double bind. Schools are criticized for not changing, and for some of the changes they have made in the past. Demands are not accompanied by supports, whether financial or political. This helps to explain the frustration that was often expressed, as well as the common plea for clearer provincial direction, political and financial support, and a more coherent and consistent approach to public education.

I also feel that there frequently does not seem to be a clear sense of direction from the government on down. Most of our directions are set by [the provincial government] and they vacillate from year to year. I think that causes a lot of confusion.

The clientele that we deal with has also changed. We are seeing more violence, more transient students in our schools and more disintegration within the family. We are seeing students that just do not have family supports such as were in place even ten years ago. We are dealing with a lot of social, societal factors. (Rural district school administrator)

Ambivalence about change is linked to uncertainty about the implications of social change for the role of schools. In many areas our colleagues are wondering what the role of the school is. However this concern emerges in quite different ways depending on the specific issue. Though technological change, labour force change and changes in families all pose challenges to schools, our colleagues think about them in rather different ways, as we will show in later chapters.

These three rough sets of attitudes toward social change — resentment, ambivalence and opportunism — reflect what our colleagues said in the interviews. Readers should be careful about any further inferences or judgments. For one thing, none of our colleagues were indifferent to social change. Many of them spoke passionately about change, even though their thinking took quite different directions. For another, while we ourselves are inclined to see many of the challenges of social change as educational opportunities, this does not mean that we believe that the concerns of people who resent social change or are ambivalent about it are somehow reactionary or ill-founded. Quite the contrary. Their caution, as well as their concern for social continuity and stability, will turn out to be constructive in the long run. Many of our colleagues have worked very hard to create an improved political climate, to put their systems on a sound financial footing, or to balance the interests of various communities and interest groups.

Over time, it seems likely that the nature and processes of schooling will be determined as much by people who have not yet embraced change as by people who are now its enthusiastic proponents. If for no other reason than this, there is a need for sympathetic understanding of their views.

Note

1 The terminology around Aboriginal people in Canada is complex. The word 'Indian' refers only to persons who are registered under the Indian Act of Canada, which regulates relations between the national government and the various tribes that signed treaties. The various Indian bands on reserves across Canada describe themselves as First Nations, which would include status Indians as well as other people connected to the band but who don't have legal Indian status. 'Aboriginal' is a broader term that takes in people who may not be Indians legally, but think of themselves as having an Indian or Inuit (Eskimo) background of some kind. Other terms sometimes used are 'native', which is more or less synonymous with Aboriginal, and Metis, which refers to people whose ancestors included both Indians and Europeans. Many complicated issues of legal status, treaty rights, self-governance rights and land claims are currently being worked out with various Aboriginal groups.

Chapter 4

Learning About the Changing World

This chapter is about learning — the ways in which our colleagues acquired their knowledge of and ideas about the changing social context for their work and for schools generally.

In Chapter 1 we provided a very brief discussion of learning in organizations. Although the idea of organizational learning is attractive, achieving learning in real organizations is difficult because the issues are complex, human capacity to deal with complexity is quite limited, and people do not necessarily agree on what issues are most important or what their implications are. The structure of hierarchical organizations, such as school systems, may work against learning processes. All of these limitations pose challenges for schools in understanding the changing world around them.

Nor do humans necessarily have a predilection for learning. Lindblom (1990), examining the historical record, puts it starkly:

> The whole history of humankind reads in some large part as a history of impairment of inquiry: ignorance, superstition, barriers to inquiry, exile and execution of dissenters, the many intimidations of tyranny, illiteracy, the steady impositions of peer pressure, and the use of media for propaganda, among many manifestations. (Lindblom, p. 69)

We also note that learning is a political process, something which tends to be underplayed in the organizational learning literature. This poses a dilemma: that while learning is political, the nature of politics is changing. Learning *through* political processes also means learning *about* emerging political processes, which strikes us as something akin to trying to measure something with instruments that are themselves changing.

Keeping in mind these barriers and limits to effective learning in organizations, let us now turn to the processes for learning about the external world in the school systems we studied. As described in the previous chapter, our colleagues were keenly aware of the many external pressures affecting their school systems, and had first hand experience with many specific, local instances of social change.

In our view, the ways school systems learn about social change may be suitable for understanding the local manifestations of change, but seem unlikely to help people achieve the bigger picture they need and want. Individuals are often thoughtful and outward-looking, but the school systems themselves were generally not. The ways that problems are addressed, that information is generated, that ideas are circulated, and that meaning is cultivated seem more likely to lead to a fragmented than to a coherent understanding of the emerging place of education in a changing world. As we suggested in the previous chapter, social change tends to be seen as interfering with the work of schooling rather than being seen as the backdrop that should give education its meaning and focus.

The learning processes of school systems, like other organizations, are necessarily both social and sociological. They are undertaken with other people as well as shaped by the institutional structures and professional relationships which mark school systems. However we believe that the former aspect is too prominent and that organizational structure for learning is generally underdeveloped in schools.

Sources of Information

Our colleagues told us that the districts rely for their understanding primarily on the experiences and initiatives of individuals. Within the school this means the direct experience of teachers and principals as they encounter students and parents. This seemed to reinforce the tendency to understand external pressures in terms of their local, concrete manifestations, without a larger framework for interpreting their experiences.

> In our school we became more aware that it was happening as a result of a change in our school population; the number of ESL kids, for example, that we had coming into our school, the range of languages they were speaking and the parts of the world that they were coming from.
> We tend to do it in an informal way. It happens as a result of dealing every day with kids of diverse ethno-cultural backgrounds in school. We cannot do that without talking about the larger issues that are impacting not only on our local community, but on our country and maybe on the global community. We cannot ignore the fact that we have kids coming to school who are on welfare or have single mothers. We have to talk about those larger issues as a result of having those students here. It comes about, not in structured way. (Suburban district school administrator)

At the district level the processes are less direct, but also informal and generally poorly developed, relying a great deal on the initiatives of individuals, on informal gatherings of staff, and on whatever professional development opportunities are available.

How do we identify [issues]? Deal with them? Cope with them? In our district a number of strategies. One of the simplest ones is that we send teachers out to conferences so that they learn to identify these ideas and concepts. We also have working groups within the district such as the principals' working group and the [teachers' association], and they meet frequently. If, for instance, a principal attends a conference where he learns about a new piece of software, he then brings that information back and shares it with the other principals in the group. Then, to make it effective, there are innovative and creative teachers who can transform these ideas into classroom implementation. At that point teacher groups get together and exchange information. There is a dynamic which circulates information within the district on an ongoing basis. (Urban district school board member)

The administrator gives us information, and, along with staff, we attend a few conferences and workshops. We also have meetings with the principal, and the teachers send us brochures. So that is how we keep in touch. Our administrator is very good, and we have a lot of interaction with other people. (Aboriginal district school board member)

Arrangements for organizational learning are non formal and seen as an activity for individuals, not the organization itself. Systems don't appear to devote significant attention or time to methodical scanning or exploration of their environments.

Question What are your sources of information?
[The school trustees'] magazine. Also, a regular mailing of national magazines or a news collection that the administration receives and sends out to trustees. Trustees in [this district] are reluctant to go out to conferences, however they do sometimes attend. We mainly rely on people for whom we provide leaves to attend conferences, and we require their reports. We listen to television, radio, read the newspaper, and discuss issues with the public. (Urban district school board member)

We mentioned in Chapter 3 that official district documents, such as school board or senior administrative minutes, showed few mentions of discussion of important external issues. Our colleagues generally confirmed this in the interviews.

Perhaps in some ways we are our own worst enemy because we haven't put the processes in place to develop our own focus. We don't have a mechanism that links the purpose of district with the policies and programs, and because we lack this we are more susceptible to being distracted by other issues. If you think of the school district as a tree, and our work as the branches, when issues came along we put them on a branch. If we had a better framework we could know which branch to hang each issue on and be better able to work through the issues. (Urban district administrator)

The processes that are typically connected in the literature to organizational learning — research, data analysis and structured discussion of issues — play a small role in these districts. Formal research, when mentioned at all, was in the context of particular issues, usually as the role of study groups or as part of local review processes. The research was always done by some other person or group. No distinction was made between research as part of the learning process, and research as an element of formulating a response to an issue. The urban district was the only one to have staff officially devoted to research, and the superintendent was at pains to point out that the branch didn't really do 'research', in the sense of undertaking a careful analysis of local trends in the light of some larger theoretical framework, but instead collected 'information'.

> **Question** How important a role does research play in helping to set the agenda?
> I guess on a five point scale, probably in the middle. We don't generate research. We have a research department to generate information, not research. The research we get is from individuals, or study groups with members of the administration, and from reading. Research is not a huge factor. We deal more with the immediate realities, or the realities we think we're going to face further down the road. Our Research Department has only about 1½ professional people. (Urban district administrator)

A number of colleagues did, however, report professional reading as one of the influences on them.

> Okay, there are a number of ways I become aware of things — one is the regular bulletins that come out from the Department of Education, and the [teachers' organization]. We receive all these, even though we are not a provincial school. They send us information announcing a new curriculum and new curriculm guides. For broader issues in education, I get most of my information from my own reading in journals. I am a member of the Association for Supervision and Curriculum Development based in the United States of America. They are an excellent resource. (Aboriginal district administrator)

The media were reported by our colleagues to play a minor role in shaping their world view. The media were frequently described as persistently critical of education ('education bashing' was the phrase we heard most often). Some of our colleagues mentioned them as a source of information, and in this way they may have helped to set the agenda of school systems. But this is where their influence was said to have ended.

> **Question** What role do the media play in shaping the decisions about education?
> I don't think they play a very big role at all. The [older local newspaper] has attempted to provide some information. The [newer local newspaper] just finds fault and wants to show only the bad side of education. The television media is not a factor. (Urban district administrator)

We are somewhat sceptical about this limited view of the role and impact of the media in contemporary life, and are inclined to see them as more influential than some of our colleagues may think. This may be especially so for school board members, who after all are in political roles, so that the public mood as reflected in the media is important.

> We read the papers, watch the news, and we also get a lot of material from the board office. We attend conferences, too . . .
> The other good thing that started happening recently in our district is that our local paper has been giving us a lot of positive comments. It feels nice to pick up the paper and read that there is something the schools are doing which is good. (Suburban-rural school board member)

Though many of our colleagues are critical of the way the media portray education, their own views on particular issues such as those discussed in later chapters often seem to echo opinions expressed in the media. It is possible that the role of the media is less direct than we think, or that the media themselves are simply reflecting wider trends that also influence our colleagues. The whole area of media influences on thinking about education is one that needs more examination.

How Social Change becomes Salient to School Systems

Our data suggest that much of the learning in school systems about external change is incidental, or concerned with immediate local problems. To have an impact on a system, however, an issue needs to be noticed and learning about the issue needs to be integrated into the networks and connections that make up the system as well as seen as part of the process of creating the bigger picture in the district.

Noticing issues is more than being aware of them. An issue that has been noticed is one that is to be taken seriously whether as a focal point of policy making or as a factor to be taken into account when making other decisions.

It may be placed in the foreground, as an issue to be dealt with in its own right on the system's agenda. It might also lie in the background, as something to be considered when other problems are being addressed.

Our colleagues acknowledged that they made decisions about which issues were important, but they had difficulty articulating what issues they took notice of, as well as when.

The legitimacy conferred by provincial policy and financial support is particularly important in determining formal agenda items for school systems. Anything passed down by the Department of Education is likely to appear on district agendas regardless of the district's own view of the measure. Other issues become salient to districts because of changes in provincial law or policy, or because of public commissions of inquiry.

The issue of pay equity is an initiative basically by the government. The districts were asked to look at it and were encouraged to do so by the province providing half the funding for the implementation of it. (Suburban district administrator)

We should take some of the [provincial government] directives with a grain of salt. An example might be workplace regulations for noise level in the workplace. When it came out, our district went to great lengths and expense to comply with their requests. Now, we discover that we are one of only two school districts to have done so. Sometimes the standards are designed for industry, but we are asked to adopt them. These things take up a lot of our energy and time in non-productive ways. Workplace safety committees are another example. (Suburban-rural district administrator)

Setting Priorities

In addition to making some decisions about the issues they would attend to, our colleagues also made decisions about the importance of various external changes. As suggested in Chapter 3, even when an issue is widely seen as important, people within a district may have quite different views as to the appropriate response. A provincial initiative to review school district boundaries is an interesting example. Many people saw the review of school district boundaries as a major source of uncertainty in the system, some chose to proceed with business as usual, while others delayed action until the commission reported, and then waited for the government to decide whether to act on the Commission's sweeping recommendations. In the end the government shelved the report, meaning that for some districts important developments had been unnecessarily put aside for three years.

Whether speaking of their choices of issues or the meaning they attached to issues once they decided to pursue them, our colleagues had difficulty speaking about the criteria they used. These criteria had to be inferred from the way they compared their approaches to various issues.

Question There are so many issues that are potentially on the table, how does the board and the system come to some sense of which ones that we really have to deal with, and these are the ones we'll deal with later?
In other words, how does the board set priorities. The board and the administration have criteria and one of the basic criteria is what's best for the children. Another criterion is can we afford it. Another basis would be parental pressures. When we have long line-ups for enrollment in alternative programs that provides a pressure that causes new programs to develop. Another criterion is the initiatives of teachers. (Urban district school board member)

Question How does an issue that is primarily of concern at the level of the school get transformed into something that becomes more apparent district wide? Is it just as its incidence increases?
I think it becomes of concern as its incidence increases and the people at the school level pass that concern on to the administrative level through the ongoing discussions that we have with our administrators and our school based people. We keep hearing a pervasive message and it kind of works its way up through the system. Parents and teachers make issues known to trustees. Liaison meetings with employees are a vehicle. (Suburban district school board member)

This discussion with a school board member went on to talk about the differences in the way two issues — poverty and technology — were seen in the district. We quote it at length to show these differences.

Question What about technology? What is its state and did it work its way up through the system in the same fashion?
It worked its way up that way, but there were a lot of outside forces too. It was probably one issue in which we got a lot of feedback from parents who have major concerns because they are seeing the need and the growing technology within their own workplaces. We are getting it both ends; from the parents, from the community and also from the system as a whole. We are responding very positively in [the district]. One of our board priorities is the whole area of technology ... We have some pretty innovative initiatives going on in some of our schools ... It is something that is very visible within the district.

Question There is more enthusiasm for technology than for poverty, more urgency, it seems. Perhaps enthusiasm is not quite the right word, perhaps more urgency ...

That is probably a fair statement. Why is that so? I would suspect that maybe the whole issue of poverty is still somewhat new to the majority of [the district]. Maybe it is an issue that is a little more difficult to deal with; maybe a little more sensitive, perhaps not as visible as technology. I would hate to say it is less important and I don't think that at a basic level it would be considered less important than technology. Maybe technology is something that generally we feel that we can do something more tangible, the sort of thing we know how to attack and what to do about it.

. . . I wonder sometimes whether the whole issue of poverty becomes so evident in some areas that you are almost forced to do something about it. Whereas in other areas where it is in small pockets, you know it's there, but it is not so evident and hitting you in the face, you are not getting that constant bombardment about trying to do something about it . . . Do we react as a system and as a process to the squeaky wheel? I think that does happen.

To my mind the explanation for that difference between the district approach and the local approach is that we see technology as being part of education, a responsibility of the educational system. Poverty is tied in with the community, it's more of a community type problem. (Suburban district school board member)

Connections and Linkages

School system administrators and politicians develop networks and relationships with internal and external groups and agencies for a variety of reasons: to secure their support and cultivate their confidence, to exchange information, to ensure enough consistency among districts that unfavorable comparisons are not made, and to maintain a sense of connection to the outside world.

There are networks within each school system and some connections across systems. Administrators play particularly important linking roles.

The board is very cautious about raising taxes because there are always comparisons being drawn . . . The effect of the current situation is that you get a lot of comparison among the different districts, and the local school trustees feel that they shouldn't put too much of a tax burden on their constituents. (Rural district administrator)

I think there is a very good network set up in the district whereby information gets to the board, and information from the board flows back to the administrators, principals, and so on. Teachers also make presentations to the board on a frequent basis. There is a very good working relationship in the district. (Aboriginal district administrator)

I serve as a liaison between the board and other organizations, other school boards, other superintendents, community members. Most correspondence comes through me. If anything is going on I usually here about it and let the board know, and they decide what they're going to do. (Suburban-rural district administrator)

Forging linkages with other organizations is seen as important.

We also recognize that in a rural community, the education system plays a major role in the cultural and economic development of the area. In that role as corporate citizen and partner in the economic prosperity of the community, the school district has representation on the Chamber of Commerce [and other community organizations]. (Suburban-rural district administrator)

One of the pieces of advice that I have found useful over the years is socializing with people outside of education, with people from other professions and the business world. They have a better chance to understand where you are coming from as an educator and you have a better chance to understand where they are coming from as government employees, or representatives of the business sector or the private sector. (Suburban district administrator)

Creating networks is easier in small communities.

One of the major factors for our school is that we are a very small community. Most of the staff live in the community. Most of the community went to school in the school district and know the administrators and the teachers and how the system works. Many of our staff are involved in the community like the Chamber of Commerce. As a side note, for the third time in the last few years, our citizen of the year last year is a former staff member. Because it is a smallish community and because we have co-operative education and work experience, the public feel very comfortable coming in if there is a major concern. It is not just to complain or grumble about something or other, they will come in with a major idea and say what do you think about it? Can it work? They will sit down and talk about it. That relationship has been very positive. (Suburban-rural school administrator)

Yet working across institutional boundaries seems to be very difficult in all settings.

We find it very difficult to work with outside agencies in the school system. We started a group working with the mental health area. It got nowhere because they were not willing to discuss problems that were within the community. They would not discuss cases. If we had a case in the school that we thought would be better handled in discussion with them, they would not have anything to do with it. It just fell apart . . .

The only outside agency with which we have had any success is Child and Family Services. We have an agreement to share a worker with them. That is working quite well after a couple of initial rocky years. They share back and forth with us. Other agencies know the problem. We have met with the [police] corporal here and they know the problem but they do not seem to be willing to face it. (Rural district administrator)

And school systems have not necessarily been very open or willing to change on their own.

Yes, not only do we not look outside we also do not invite others to look at us. We do not invite others to come in even though we acknowledge there are some significant others like parents. We do not ask the kids to work through the dilemmas with us. As soon as we have dilemmas we push them (the kids) behind closed doors. We also do not take advantage of all the learning experiences that can benefit the kids. (Suburban district administrator)

Internal change? I'm trying to think of something that's been. It's almost as though there is so much busy work that many develop an attitude that resists change because it is difficult and intense. As a result, most of the programs are initiated externally. (Urban district school board member)

Moreover, the community pressures are divergent and so they make matters more complex, not less.

Well, let me refer to some of our critics, to whom we do need to listen. Some of them do not place the same value on social or cooperation skills. When we talk with people from large business, they say they want people with good social skills, communication skills, problem solving and cooperation skills. When we talk to people from small business, they are saying that they want people with specific employable skills. Then there is a group of people who want to go back to the basics, who follow the military 'It is not for you to question why, but to do or die.' There is still that element out there. We can not cater to all these goals because they are not compatible. (Suburban district administrator)

Getting the 'Big Picture'

For nearly all of our colleagues getting the 'big picture' was an important priority, even though they differed greatly in how and where that picture was to be found. They brought different and ultimately contradictory meanings to the phrase, 'the big picture'. For some the big picture was the same as vision, outward looking perhaps, but internally determined. For others it was a sense that their efforts had some positive connection to developments in the larger society, a perception that they were somehow working with social change rather than against it. And for still others it was a feeling that their efforts would be consistent with those of other systems in the province. In their minds, school systems themselves were part of the big picture and learning about external social change inevitably drew attention to their inner worlds. Their view of the big picture included the relationships of school systems to their social environments and the ability of school systems to adapt to social change.

At least some of our colleagues are well aware of the problems involved in developing a coherent view of what was happening around them. They struggled with these questions.

> We do talk about it a lot, but we don't have a grasp of how to deal with it. (Urban district administrator)

> I guess the biggest question is the how. How do we get from where we are to where we want to be? The process is so important. I find that because things are changing in spite of us, the resistance to change is growing. There are some changes that I would really like to see but I have difficulty with how to do it, how to make it happen without the backlash that would make it counterproductive. (Suburban district administrator)

Some saw the problem of the big picture in system-wide terms, with none of the parts of the system having begun to come to grips with the issues.

> We talk about the pressures and expectations being applied to education and I think we need to be very clear about where we think we're going with education and why we want to go there and how we're going to get there. We don't do enough of that planning. The provincial government hasn't done very much of that, the districts haven't done much of that, and I think that the schools don't do enough of that either. I'm talking the big picture. (Suburban-rural district administrator)

Several shared the view that the provincial government had special responsibilities.

I also feel that there frequently does not seem to be a clear sense of direction from the government on down. Most of our directions are set by [the department of education] and they vacillate from year to year. I think that causes a lot of confusion. (Rural district school administrator)

But others believed that they themselves had responsibilities in this area.

I don't think we do a very good job (of getting the big picture). I think that in the schools in particular we have a very narrow focus. . . . I mentioned before that we're paying the price of dropouts, we're seeing them now as parents, who for whatever reason chose not to finish high school and are now unemployable. I think that we're so focused on students, programs, and local issues that we're not very good at seeing the larger issues. (Suburban-rural district administrator)

We spend quite a bit of time meeting to discuss how we are going to accomplish what we have to do over the next few weeks. We spend time on how board policy and finances will impact on the district. We do spend a lot of time on managing the system. What we don't spend enough time on is the vision for the system, where we are going, how what I'm doing affects what other districts are doing. It would take a more concerted effort from all of us here to set aside some of the time that gets spent in management issues and put it into long-term planning. (Urban district administrator)

For some, the beginnings were inside school systems, asking 'bigger questions'.

There have been changes in the classroom, such as technology and changes in approaches to teaching, that reflect changes in society such as goals and values, whether its vocational education, or behavior management programs. Does school reflect society, or does society reflect school? I'm never sure of the answer to that. Those kinds of things change constantly. It's good that societal pressures do impact on schools and that schools have to respond. The biggest question coming out of these issues is can the school system truly provide leadership in a society where there is so much change or is it always in the position of having to react to some other agenda? My feeling is that the school district should be providing more leadership than it is, and that it tends to be more reactive than proactive. (Urban district administrator)

In whatever way the big picture is developed, the isolation of work in schools and school systems will have to be overcome.

[T]he more narrow you are, the less you are likely to learn about (the changes). Part of the problem is that we have teachers scheduled to be in this little box for these many hours and then maybe to do some preparation to be in that little box tomorrow, and then fit their personal life around that. Teachers do not have the advantage that we [administrators] have — to do the reading, reflect with colleagues, grapple with the dilemmas.

I think the teachers need to know more about the real world, what goes on outside education. All of us get entrenched in the world we are in, and I think we all need to look beyond and have some experience outside. We need work experience for teachers, not just kids. We need to listen to people who work in other environments. We are not preparing kids to be teachers. (Suburban district administrator)

Learning About Social Change: Some Reflections

There were many obstacles and constraints to learning about social change in our partner districts. The systems, in our colleagues' view, lacked effective ways for learning about the big picture, for integrating its various elements, and then for linking what they have learned to policies and practices. School systems are preoccupied with their inner worlds and consequently have difficulty understanding change in wider terms. The strategies used for learning about social change are limited. Virtually all connections between school systems and other organizations are at administrative and political levels and so do not address the isolation of schools and teachers that so many of our colleagues mentioned. We found little organized effort to mobilize the diversity and vitality implied by a participatory understanding of responding to social change, where power is shared, learning activity is collaborative, and leadership is widespread. There is something ironic about school systems that have learning as their aim, but are not themselves organized for it.

While better organization would make some difference from a learning point of view, the real difficulties may well be meta-cognitive as much as organizational. To see the world differently may require changing how we think. Browning (1991) has suggested that an institution's internal workings take their meaning from larger narratives about the institution's place in the world. The narratives provide archetypes, or larger plots, for the stories of individual school systems. Similarly, in *The Fifth Discipline* Senge (1990) points to the importance of the epistemological assumptions and organizational forms that dominate our society.

From a very early age, we are taught to break apart problems, to fragment the world. This apparently makes complex tasks and subjects more manageable, but we pay an enormous hidden price. We can no longer see the consequences of our actions; we lose our intrinsic sense of connection to the larger whole. When we then try to 'see the big picture' we try to reassemble the fragments in our minds, to list and organize the pieces . . . the task is futile . . . similar to trying to reassemble the fragments of a broken mirror to see a true reflection. (Senge, p. 11)

An even more pessimistic assessment comes from anthropologist Mary Douglas (1986), who believes that organizations inevitably restrict what their members can or will see and consider.

Institutions systematically direct individual memory and channel our perceptions into forms compatible with the relations they authorize. They fix processes that are essentially dynamic, they hide their influence, and they rouse our emotions to a standardized pitch on standardized issues. Add to all this that they endow themselves with rightness and send their mutual corroboration cascading through all the levels of our information system . . . Any problems we try to think about are automatically transformed into their own organizational problems. The solutions they proffer only come from the limited range of their experience . . . Institutions have the pathetic megalomania of the computer whose whole vision of the world is its own program. (Douglas, p. 92)

If these writers are correct — if the problems in finding the big picture are rooted in our culture and are not simply traceable to the present social and political organization of school — school systems may be in for a long period of uncertainty.

However, such uncertainty is not inevitable. The Aboriginal school district was especially interesting in this respect. Not only is the district culturally and historically different from our other partner districts, it was the only district of the five to have a clearly and widely understood story of itself. The story is one of the absolute belief in the importance of education to the community, and of the community's wresting control of education from the federal government. There is a conviction that, no matter how great the present difficulties, things are now better than they were not very long ago. That story explains what they do — especially, it explains them to themselves.

. . . the situation is improving as people get educated. Students still drop out in Grades 8 and 9 but we are accomplishing what the Department of Indian Affairs could never accomplish — graduates. We graduated thirteen people in June and that has been the average for the past ten years. For the first ten years we did not have many graduates but we have been in local control for twenty years and the graduate list is increasing every year, whereas under Indian Affairs [this community] had one graduate in fifty years. (Aboriginal district administrator)

Although we think organizations do need some big picture to be effective, we must confess to some reservations about the motives which seem to underlie our colleagues' search for the big picture. We know that our colleagues have an authentic desire to find a place for themselves and their systems in a rapidly changing world. Nevertheless, relatively few of them saw positive opportunities for schools arising from social change. Some of our colleagues expressed a sense of loss. Others were frustrated that the systems they had spent their careers building were now being dismantled. Most, though, spoke of what they wanted, but didn't have: direction, coherence, a sense of order, reduced conflict and uncertainty, a clearer perception of the role and social function of schools, security of place. All in all, a condition that is considerably more intelligible and reassuring than the situation in which they now find themselves.

But what if no such condition exists? What if the big picture turns out to be fragmented and incoherent? What then?

> In the work of trying to understand, disorder and incoherence are more probable. Whenever a high degree of logic and complexity is found, it is a matter for surprise and needs to be explained . . . A truly complex ordering is the result of sustained effort . . . in the absence of inducements for specialized concentration, classification will meet minimum needs by taking the path of least effort. (Douglas, 1986, p. 56)

And what if there is more than one big picture possible? This seems to us to be a more hopeful situation — if we can turn uncertainty to advantage. For instance, the vagueness of educational goals is now a topic of much complaint. It is said that vague goals impede planning because they are too abstract to guide decision making. They create high expectations which, when not met, are a source of frustration. On the other hand, vague goals can give institutions more autonomy and flexibility, and make compromise and integration easier. Vague goals enhance the elasticity of an institution, and thus its ability to accommodate future change. There are advantages to vague as well as clearly defined goals, just as there is a price to be paid for each.

We don't believe that there is only one 'big picture' emerging, or that the social changes which are now occurring are evenly paced and distributed. Nor are we convinced that one big picture is really necessary or, for that matter, desirable. Most of our colleagues have a very positive view of education in the last forty years, and see the big picture of the period as one of considerable progress. But such an interpretation of the recent past ignores, if not denies, other parts of the story, for example: racial and class conflict, the plight of Aboriginal Canadians, the experience of immigrants, the difficulties of labor, or the decline of rural communities. The search for a usable big picture might, like the writing of school history textbooks, become simply an instrument of the dominant interests of the day. Whose big picture, and for what purposes, are critical questions?

To find the intellectual keys to respond appropriately to social change, we need to broaden, not narrow, how we think of education and social change. There are countless ways in which school systems might think about and respond positively to social change. We explore some of these throughout this book. At least for the present we might be better served not by seeking a grand new pattern for education, but by engaging in the kind of thinking and experimentation from which, if it is still wanted, that new pattern might eventually be drawn. Learning about social change must become an essential part of what schools do.

Chapter 5

How School Systems Respond to Social Change

In previous chapters we have focused on the ways in which people in school systems understand and learn about issues. We now turn our attention to the ways that school systems are trying to respond to social change — the actions they are taking in light of their understanding. Processes of learning and understanding are vital, but must be connected to action if they are to make any difference. It is easy to have good intentions if one doesn't act on them.

Although school systems have always had to cope with social change, the present seems to be a very different moment. The context for responding to change has shifted, and with it apparently the ability of school systems to harmonize social change with prevailing ideas about the nature and structure of education. It is partly a matter of a mismatch between old styles of problem solving and new problems, and partly a matter of optimism, confidence and personal efficacy. Even if people were to acquire new problem solving skills, they are not sure they like the shape of the emerging future or the place of schools in it, they are not confident that they will be able to acquire the financial resources and public support they believe they need, and, in an atmosphere of increasing regulation at the provincial level and decreasing willingness to be led at the community level, they are not clear how much difference their own views and positions make.

In the forty years between 1950 and 1990, school systems in most countries expanded enormously — in enrollments, in the size of institutions, in the resources available to operate them, in the scope and variety of programs, in personnel. Population growth alone is not an adequate explanation: there were profoundly important economic and social reasons for the expansion and educators, not surprisingly, rode the crests of their waves.

As we noted in Chapter 1, in industrialized countries today public educational systems are shrinking, not expanding. Social change continues, but there is a marked contrast in how educators now think of social change. Most of our colleagues believe that public education is under siege. Many feel impotent in the face of social change and powerless to direct the school systems' response. Nearly all of them were uncertain what social change would bring to school systems. Many wonder about the continuing relevance of schools, at least as we have known them. What accounts for this shift in attitude and loss of confidence?

There are several partial explanations. One is that change has had a negative impact on some people. Changing priorities, values and personal frames of reference is never easy. Some people believe that changing an organization's structure or approach devalues past accomplishments. Some of the old skills are no longer required, and it's easier to find people with new skills rather than to retrain people.

Another lies in the tempo of change as well as the number and intensity of social changes occurring simultaneously. Although the various social changes are not necessarily linked, their cumulative impact is very great. Setting priorities is difficult. People are quite simply off balance or overwhelmed, and don't know how or where to begin. In such circumstances, it should not be surprising that people turn inwards, temporize, or fall back on what they know.

A further explanation is that old assumptions die hard. Most of the concepts and theories for dealing with change developed in a period of expansion and at a time when there was greater deference to political and professional authority. What Schon (1971) termed 'ideas in good currency' have changed in education. Expansion has given way to contraction and retrenchment, and the political climate has certainly changed. Old strategies of responding to change may no longer be appropriate or adequate. Additional resources are unavailable, which means that new priorities must be addressed by the reallocation of existing resources, a process that is very difficult at the best of times. Our colleagues recognize this, but are not necessarily sure of how to respond.

> We went through a period when we felt secure that funding was available, and that we could offer the programs we wanted, as well as develop new programs. This period began in the 1960s. The period of restraint began in the early 1980s. Basically, restraint means that the things we want to acquire, purchase and value, we are not always able to get. A great deal of our emphasis now is placed on prioritizing, and on downsizing. In the past, you didn't have to prioritize, or if you did prioritize, you were prioritizing items or services that you planned to add to the system. . . . (Then) we were used to having the funding to put into place any initiative that we saw fit, but now it has limited us quite a bit in those areas. I think we've been able to undertake some initiatives, but we've had to scale down our plans and our dreams. (Suburban district administrator)

We have observed that internal matters dominate the agendas of school districts, and systematic discussions of external change are neglected. Strategic decision making is difficult. Districts have many, often conflicting goals. Educators feel overwhelmed by the range and force of pressures facing them. There is a lack of consensus on what forces are most important and on what to do about them. Districts are not proactive in reading the environment. Given obstacles and learning incapacities as well as the absence of a 'big picture' (all discussed at greater length in Chapter 4), it should not be too surprising that the responses of our partner districts to social changes tended to be ad hoc, opportunistic, and highly decentralized, with a strong emphasis on voluntary initiatives at the school level. West and Hopkins (1995), in studying the experience of British schools with self-management, found

> . . . the majority of schools are unprepared to exercise control over their own futures. They simply do not have the structures, the experience or the strategies necessary to move the school systematically in a given direction, even where there is increased clarity about what the direction should be. (West and Hopkins, 1995, p. 8)

Basic Approaches to Responding to Change

One group of our colleagues is not very oriented to responding to social change. They believe that they are doing the best they can under increasingly difficult circumstances; that present educational structures and processes are basically sound, though somewhat starved financially. Another group recognizes that schools will need to change, but does not yet have a strong sense of what the changes will be or how they will come about.

Yet these differences in basic views did not seem reflected in different strategies for change. The basic pattern was similar across all our partner districts and in our survey data. Their responses were realistic adjustments to local social changes, shaped by local trends, conflicts, political traditions, and financial realities — but piecemeal. Self-reassurance rather than self-examination is the mode, even for activities that ostensibly were intended to lead to change. Issues are usually seen as hard choices within present frameworks, not as opportunities to rethink the meaning and nature of public education.

Many changes are being supported, but they tend to be approached concretely, and one at a time. Schools rely on a limited set of practices to support change, and most of those practices imitate the current situation. For example, when new needs or issues are identified the initial response is to use existing strategies such as adding specialized staff, or developing new curricula. Their explorations moved them sideways rather than forward, contributing to the diversification of existing programs and activities but not to the creation of new ideas about the nature and processes of education.

A frequent response to perceived pressure was a school-based 'project'. Most of these seemed, from the outside at least, to be isolated from other projects and not linked to larger ideas about the development of education in the district. Although there is much innovation in terms of curriculum or teaching methods, much of it appears to have little lasting effect on teaching and learning, often because one initiative is soon superseded by another, and few of them are adequately supported either with opportunities for teachers to learn, practice and incorporate changes into their daily work or with the structural changes that would be required to make them an ongoing part of the organization (Cohen, 1992; Cuban, 1990).

A particularly interesting feature of change in schools is reliance on volunteers — on committed teachers or administrators who take on additional tasks voluntarily. As a result, many changes are not institutionalized and may die if key staff leave.

> I guess it is the grassroots, otherwise we wouldn't be able to cope. I don't see a federal initiative or a federal goal in education. The support at the provincial level is decreasing. There is less support from the Department of Education. There is a lot of turmoil and instability, cost-saving measures and so forth. We have tried to accomplish as much as possible from within the district. You find that you rely on staff all the way through. We sponsor special area groups and study groups from within the district and they provide good ideas. (Suburban-rural district school board member)

These practices are illustrated in the next few chapters in which we look at the ways school systems respond to particular issues. For example, responses to labor market change involved such strategies as expanding guidance and counseling services or adding additional courses in areas such as co-operative education. Partnerships with external organizations, which did represent a new approach to education, tended still to be rather limited in scope. In regard to technology, the focus has been on the acquisition of hardware and software to be used within a conventional approach to school organization, teaching and learning. In the case of poverty, schools focused on additional services for students seen as needy rather than on overall changes in organization and instruction. As March (1991) suggests,

> Schools and other educational institutions have invested rather little in absorptive capacity . . . they have the capability of using new ideas that are close to their existing technologies, but they have not built an inventory of prior knowledge that would permit them to use radically new ideas intelligently. As a result, they tend to adopt the form but not the substance of new concepts. (March, 1991, p. 29)

The Gap Between Problem and Solution

Paradoxically, many of our colleagues were aware that the strategies they were using seemed inadequate to the problems they saw themselves facing.

Question How well do you think we do as educators, as an educational system in trying to stay outward-looking and in touch with those kinds of shifts that are going on around us?

How well do we do? At times we do very well, at other times we are out of it completely. I guess it would depend on certain issues; how quickly we recognize that to be a factor in education, and once we recognize that, how quickly we are able to identify some ways of dealing with it. I think that overall, within the last twenty years we have fared fairly well given all the changes that have occurred. 'Fairly well' is a relative term. We could have done much better, I have no doubts about it . . . (Suburban district administrator)

One of the reasons we find ourselves in trouble today is that the public school system has been maintained as an unchanging constant, a solid anchor that has now reached a point where the boat it is holding is moving away from the anchor, because the current and everything else around it are totally different now from what they were when the system was just established. We are now in a post-industrial society with all kinds of different needs. Employment is not guaranteed any more, society is no longer able to meet its obligations to those who are less able, financial resources are dwindling, and technology is impacting our daily lives in numerous ways. The public school system has a mandate to continue what it has always done, but I think that will be unable to do this without being totally restructured, and without having the community try and have some vision of the type of education it wants for the future generation. (Urban district school administrator)

Additional information about the disjuncture between what is seen as needed and what is actually being done comes from our survey data. We asked respondents for each of the three issues — technology, labor force change and poverty — to rate a series of options for dealing with each issue in terms of their value and to indicate if each option had been implemented in their district. We examine the data on each issue in Chapters 6, 7 and 8. However a pattern across the three issues was a considerable gap between the strategies our respondents — school board members and chief superintendents — saw as potentially valuable and the strategies they reported having implemented in their own districts. In some cases the gaps were enormous, with 80 percent or more of respondents rating a strategy as effective but 50 percent or less indicating it had been implemented. Table 5.1 gives some examples of the larger gaps between strategies seen as effective and strategies actually implemented. Clearly many educators see the potential to do more than is currently being done.

Explaining the Gap

What explains this rather limited approach to responding to change? Our colleagues made a number of suggestions. Some thought that the problem lay in individual resistance to change, or comfort with the status quo.

Table 5.1: *Strategies — effective and implemented*

Issue	Strategy	% Rating Effective	% Indicating Implemented
Technology	Increase contact with other organizations using technology	85%	33%
Technology	Give students more autonomy in using technology	77%	29%
Labor force change	Teach entrepreneurship	74%	24%
Labor force change	Develop collaborative programs with post-secondary institutions	81%	25%
Poverty	Extra resources to schools with high concentrations of poor children	83%	56%
Poverty	Add supplementary programs such as meals or clothing	91%	41%

There is a general feeling that something is wrong. There are various views about where the wrong is. For some people, it is in the board office, for some it is the parents, for others it is the kids. . . . Personally I feel a tremendous amount of urgency to see some things happen that I believe are supported in research and the literature. I am impatient because they are not happening. I am not sure that applies to everybody. I think that is part of the problem — there is a big difference in the educational community about people's impressions. I think some people are comfortable where they are, and are not feeling any pressure to do anything different from what they are used to, while others are feeling tremendous pressure to do something different. (Suburban district administrator)

We mostly operate in a house keeping mode rather than projecting ahead. Although we do a little projecting, we do not do nearly enough of it. It requires time, flexible time to do it and the day to day housekeeping matters get in the way. The school board also can get in the road. (Suburban-rural district administrator)

Others spoke about the need for more planning, more research, and a more systematic approach to issues.

I think we need to move into a time where we no longer use personal opinion, and tradition — we always did it that way — as a reason for doing things. We also need to educate the non-teaching community. When you make a decision as an educator, it should be based on sound knowledge about learning and about process, not on personal opinion. (Suburban district administrator)

The education system should be doing more long-range planning. It has been extremely frustrating to learn about funding levels or resource levels at a very late date. I realize it is difficult for the province to speculate on their resource level, but I think we could better plan if we had some indication of the resource level earlier on. Our board of trustees has certainly attempted to budget in that way but, again, it is subject to the last minute identification of funding levels. Everyone from the trustees to the superintendents and to the schools gets very frustrated and they often have to alter their plans on short notice, at a time when long-term plans very often cannot be implemented. (Urban district administrator)

We suggest that although these points have merit, the pattern of response to external change in school systems is the result of a number of factors — district traditions, conflicts and political processes, the approach to planning and research, a series of structural features of schooling, and, perhaps most importantly, the overall mind set about change.

District Traditions

District traditions had an impact on the processes for responding to change, but not much of a bearing on the substance of the responses. In one district there is a strong tradition of school level as distinct from district level planning:

[This district] has a strong tradition of freedom and autonomy at the school level, and attempts to bring about greater central management have been very difficult. Not everyone recognizes that the District is ticking, and others wish the District would go away. Although I recognize that some matters are best handled at a higher level (district/provincial), I am convinced that growth and commitment to task flourish when self-imposed. (Suburban district administrator)

Another emphasizes teamwork:

I think that the biggest plus in this school district, perhaps because we are smaller, is that we really do have a team focus. A lot of it has to do with the people involved. We begin with a cup of coffee most mornings. The superintendent, secretary treasurer and the two assistants sit down, usually every morning, and strategize and plan together. I think that team work is important because the issues of program and finance are inter-related.

The school administration is another team component. We meet every second week as an administration council. All the principals come together in this group to deal with district issues such as the boundaries review and other important educational issues. That on-going contact is there. When major issues arise they are taken to admin. council, where they are thrashed out. There are no surprises and I think that's critical. A lot of the success of the administrative council has to do with the working relationships and the personalities of the people as well. (Suburban-rural district administrator)

In the urban district, community committees have come to play a major role:

Question [This district] seems to be unique in having a well-developed structure of advisory groups and parents committees and so on.

It's a major route of communication for the community direct to the Board. When I was first elected to the Board, I was telephoned by community members all the time. When the Advisory Committees started up, the number of calls I received declined. Not only are those Advisory Committees directly associated with the Board, and Board members attend the Committees on an ongoing basis, they also feed into the School Committees creating a close link between the School Committees and the Advisory Committee So, essentially, a School Committee which is managed entirely by parents, can get an idea, go through their Advisory Committee, who bring the idea to the Board. It's a lot of power and it's been well used. Administration is also thrilled with the whole idea. (Urban district school board member)

The Aboriginal and rural districts also have a particular history and way of making decisions that affects how issues get discussed. However, as we show in the next few chapters, these differences in process did not seem to lead to important differences in the substance of what was done.

Conflict and Politics

Many of the issues with which our partner districts are grappling have the potential to provoke debate and conflict. School systems are still largely at-tuned to trying to avoid or defuse conflict rather than using it as a way to learn. Skills and processes for using conflict constructively are not well developed.

There is a great resistance and there are a lot of people who have difficulty understanding when we talk about restructuring the concept of block time tabling. Restructuring requires in servicing and staff development. There is the question of time lines and the danger of a backlash resulting in a withdrawal of services. I think we are fairly happy with where we are at in [this district] but we do not want to destroy that working relationship. It is difficult to get people to accept cut backs; they expect us to come up with other solutions. (Suburban district administrator)

We have more to say about politics and conflict in Chapter 10.

Planning and Research

In the last chapter we discussed planning and research as vehicles for understanding issues, but they are also ways of developing responses to issues. A minority of colleagues spoke about planning and research in these terms. In practice, mechanisms in these areas were quite limited in all the districts, and practically non-existent in some.

For most of our colleagues, planning was a process that involved monitoring enrollment trends and staff and facility requirements, budgeting, setting annual professional development priorities, allocating resources to projects that had been proposed by school groups, and the like. It was an annual process, budget-driven but not necessarily linked to a clear set of educational objectives. Incrementalism — modest changes to an ongoing base — was the dominant approach. Formal analysis and environmental scanning were not prominent features of their work.

> We usually do a year's planning in advance and decide what kind of initiatives we're going to work on in the next year or so. Sometimes it focuses on educational initiatives. We've looked ahead to see how it would be implemented and review it after a year has gone by to see what kind of progress we've made on some of those initiatives. [Our district] certainly has had some very good educational initiatives. (Suburban district school board member)

We have already noted the strong belief in the importance of volunteers and individual initiative, with support from the system. We also heard some scepticism about the value of initiatives that did not come from within the school.

> I guess our district has a tradition of leaving many educational initiatives in the hands of educational administrators, the principals in particular. It's been a hand-off approach.
>
> **Question** Do you see that as a strength or a weakness, or both?
> In some cases it can be a strength. It encourages competition, and, in a healthy competition you can become stronger . . . There can, however, be conflicts sometimes . . . (Suburban district school board member)
>
> I am always careful about new staff coming in from other places and bringing their ideas on discipline which work well where they come

from. I always tell them the ideas are fine but we have to go very slowly and evaluate things on how they will work here instead of saying that is what works over there, so let us do it here. I appreciate teachers bringing in new ideas, but people are different, students are different. (Aboriginal district administrator)

Much the same comments might be made about the role of research. Our colleagues generally thought of research as something to be done by others, although several people did mention reflective practice as a professional ideal. Seeking solutions to local problems by turning to published research for examples and models of successful practice was typically, though not always, seen as relatively unimportant.

Structural Features of Schooling

As suggested in Chapter 1, practices in organizations such as schools are substantially influenced by existing structural and organizational features of the system that act to constrain innovation. Several of these can be mentioned as important: professional background, training and socialization; administrator selection; regulation; inconsistent goals; and the static public image of schools.

Most educators are people who liked school and were successful at it. They are not, then, oriented towards change, but towards preservation of what worked for them. Moreover, the training of teachers and administrators tends to focus on technical skills of managing the system rather than on conceptual analysis of the system or discussion of alternatives to it. Educators tend to believe that their real wisdom is found in practice, so that formal education, perhaps especially if it is unconventional, is often seen as impractical and of limited value — an irony in view of the daily commitment of educators themselves to formal education and prescribed curricula.

Administrator selection practices can also be limiting. Because schools are hierarchical in structure, promotion may depend more on pleasing one's superiors than on the demonstration of initiative. If the superiors are not very interested in change, then the group of administrators they select are unlikely to be so oriented. Empirical support for these contentions is provided by Hart (1991), who notes that the socialization of new principals is towards fitting in and not disturbing the status quo despite the rhetoric of educational leadership.

Schools also exist in a highly regulated environment. Much of what they do is shaped by restrictions or requirements placed on them by external bodies — primarily governments but also professional organizations, employers, post-secondary institutions and others. Insofar as governments require particular courses to be taught (and give national examinations on them), or universities require particular entrance requirements, or accreditation agencies expect certain configurations of staffing, the ability of schools to change is largely constrained.

One can think of schools as caught in nets or webs; no single strand may be especially strong, but the overall effect is to prevent anything from moving very much. Moreover, the strands of the web are not only physical, but become internalized by those in schools until they seem natural and inevitable. The limits may be more permeable than anyone imagines, but if they are not tested they remain real.

Establishing a clear direction for change is also difficult because schooling is an activity with multiple, sometimes inconsistent, goals and few clear outcomes. Analytical processes are hard to apply in such situations because it isn't clear what should be analysed, or from what perspective. In a given day or week a principal or superintendent will confront a bewildering array of issues: teaching and learning strategies in various subjects, changing technology, physical and sexual abuse issues, youth criminal justice provisions, cultures and patterns of adaptation by immigrants, changing political practices used by various lobby groups, medical needs of multiply handicapped children, foster parenting and child welfare policies, and so on. It is inconceivable that teachers or administrators or school board members could be knowledgeable about all the important issues facing them, since potentially, and often practically, anything and everything can turn out to be important. Yet they have somehow to cope with these issues.

A final factor that limits change is that everyone has at least some knowledge about education because all of us have gone to school. Public images of what schools are or should be are powerful influences on schools, and usually in a conservative direction. People's mental models of schooling, even for teachers, are largely shaped by one's own experience as a student. People may have strongly established ideas about what counts as a school, a classroom, a subject of study, an appropriate atmosphere, a disciplinary code. The power of these in maintaining the status quo can be very real.

> I believe change is necessary. But parents often do not support it, especially in more affluent areas. The pressure can be great, even to determining the kind of musical the school can produce . . . I've had parents objecting to changes in the layout of the school because they want the school to remain the way it was when they were students. It's a challenging task, because most people — staff, students, and parents — would like to leave everything the same. (Suburban district school administrator)

Perspectives on Change

All of these constraints are real and many of them are quite powerful. Nonetheless, the principle difficulty, as we see it, lies in the overall perspective of our colleagues towards social change. It is the basic orientation of people towards the world that affects the way they understand and respond to constraints. Our colleagues, in our view, see themselves primarily as responding to the pressures of the day, rather than as creating ways to reflect on social change, to debate educational ideas, and to forge a new approach to education. They are concerned with acceptability, while we think the present calls for imagination.

Acceptability had at least two sides for our colleagues. One looked outward, to parents, the community and 'taxpayers'. Here it meant accountability, but it included more than only frugality in the use of public resources. It also implied the need to listen to public views about education, as well as the need to create structures or processes to demonstrate that public views were considered. This helps to explain why so many of the developments mentioned by our colleagues were political and administrative rather than educational in nature. For example, the urban district restructured its governance system, to ensure greater community involvement in decisions about school and system priorities and policies. The Aboriginal district assumed control of its educational system, taking it away from the federal government. The other three districts didn't change their formal structures, but placed heavy emphasis on networking and building relationships with other organizations in their communities.

The other side of acceptability faced inward, and seemed to reflect some uncertainty about the role of senior administrators and elected officials. Were they to lead their districts somehow, or was their primary role to support the initiatives of willing volunteers? Most of our colleagues recognized this tension. While most said they did both, we've suggested that the most common strategy was to rely on school level initiatives and the projects of willing volunteers. With few exceptions, we were not able to perceive, nor were our colleagues able to articulate, a connection between the educational projects they supported and their own sense of the whole, that is, the story of education in their systems. Although our colleagues said school level proposals were wanted, even encouraged, they didn't give much indication of what they desired. The projects appeared discrete, and not linked into any overarching concepts for the development of education in the districts. We were struck by the fact that most of our partner districts had mission statements or system priorities, but these were seldom mentioned in our interviews as shaping what the districts did.

We acknowledge, as noted in Chapter 2, that our colleagues in the five school districts may well see this differently. Many felt that their systems were made up of different communities, each with different needs that could only be met in varied, local ways. This may sometimes be so, but in turn gives rise to other questions, which our colleagues also found difficult. How are differing needs such as poverty and information technology to be adjudicated? Is the district itself more than an administrative convenience, more than a conduit for funding individual schools? Why, if the communities served by schools are so different, wasn't there more diversity reported among schools?

Turning to our survey data is again helpful. After asking survey respondents about the value and use of particular strategies for each of the three issues

Table 5.2: *Barriers to Action*

Barrier	Work	Poverty	Technology
Not a major concern in our jurisdiction	3.9	3.1	4.3
Schools should not be responsible for this	3.9	3.3	4.5
Unlikely to be successful	3.8	3.0	4.5
Do not have the resources	2.9	2.3	2.8
Other issues more pressing	3.0	2.8	3.3
Provincial government does not support this area	2.5	1.9	2.5

Notes: Mean ratings — 1 = agree; 5 = disagree

(reported earlier in Table 5.1) we asked them to rate a series of obstacles or barriers to their actions. What did they see as preventing them from being more effective in dealing with these issues? Table 5.2 provides data from our respondents on the three issues expressed in terms of a mean score, with a *lower* number indicating a *more important* barrier. The most important barriers cited by our respondents were external — lack of resources and even more lack of support from the provincial government. On the whole respondents saw the issues as important, felt some responsibility for trying to deal with them, and saw possibilities for success, but felt unable to move forward as much as they might like largely because of the actions of others.

The limits of resources are very real, and during the time of our study the provincial government had been placing many other demands and pressures on schools. Our colleagues were not being misleading in citing these as important barriers. Nonetheless, it seems to us that the externalization of responsibility is indicative as much of a state of mind within the districts as it is of fiscal and political realities. Finding resources is a matter of priorities, as shown by the very significant budget allocations several districts had made to technology. Similarly, districts did feel prepared to move ahead on some issues that were important to them whether or not the province was supportive. So, while we accept that school districts do face real limits to their ability to act, limits are always related to one's mental construction of a situation. The ability to act is at least partly a function of the desire to act.

Moving Beyond Projects

We conclude this chapter by looking at the potential for more far-reaching responses to issues of social change. Could districts move beyond a project and volunteer focus for their efforts?

Projects — the voluntary initiatives of groups of parents, teachers and administrators — are to be welcomed. It is hard to imagine a school system responding to change without them. Projects have a characteristic structure which is simultaneously their principle strength and main weakness. They attract committed parents, teachers and administrators — people who are especially talented and tenacious, as well as predisposed to a certain kind of work. They emphasize a spirit of community, a feeling which fosters the ingenuity and sustains the hard practical work that projects require to be successful. But projects also operate at the edges of school systems and educational practice, and so people often find themselves marginalized or working in circumstances where what they learn is unlikely to be transferred to others.

There are many reasons why schools initiate and districts support projects; carefully exploring the possibilities of fundamental change in the nature and processes of education does not usually seem to be among them. They may function as rewards, as political symbols, or as the only alternative to an overall strategy, and they do indicate a district's vitality, for it is easy to imagine the sameness of schools without them.

The fragility of projects and the difficulty of sustaining them or replicating them on a larger scale are well known. Their existence is the product of an unusual combination of circumstances, commitment and talent. When any one of these shifts, the project itself is likely to be in jeopardy; when any one of them is not present in another setting, the project is not likely to be transferable.

But to say that projects are fragile or very hard to replicate is not to argue that they are unimportant. To the contrary. Projects, no matter how unusual the combination of circumstance, commitment and talent, demonstrate that it is possible to do something about very challenging social problems and educational issues. They can also provide a glimpse of the future, a benchmark for gauging traditional practices, and a take off point for more fundamental educational responses to social change.

The real problem with projects is the lack of overall strategic significance attached to them. Their piecemeal and idiosyncratic nature gives the impression that they are to be seen as 'only' projects, and not as fundamental experiments in the nature and processes of schooling, conducted on a system's behalf.

There is another meaning for projects which may be helpful here. It is to be found in the French term, *projet*. This term, which colloquially refers to one's long term commitments, even life's work, has no close English language equivalent. Terms such as 'vision' and 'mission' are inadequate substitutes, for they fail to convey the almost visceral engagement that the term *projet* implies. Above all, *projet* is about the big picture and the sense that one's present actions are an important part of creating a desired future. To put this another way, project is to *projet* as information is to the big picture. Just as a big picture is needed to bring coherence to pieces of information about trends that appear to be separate, it is important to see projects as part of larger, common ventures. The task is not just to undertake more or different projects, but to see them in a different way.

Coherence, it is important to underline, is not the same as consistency, and certainly doesn't imply a single or linear view of how school districts might respond to social change. Still, it is easier to say what coherence isn't than what it is. We use the term to imply a sense that ideas fit together, that conflicts can be used synergistically, that people have positive meaning for their work, and that their efforts are connected with the work of others in some mutually supportive way.

The clearest example of coherence among our partner districts was the Aboriginal school district. Perhaps coincidentally, it was also the district with the fewest discrete projects underway. Everyone in that district sees education as part of larger, vitally important social processes. They see themselves as individual participants in a larger, and valued, social project — regaining control of their own future, preserving and promoting their distinct traditions, securing their economic development. Everything that happens in the district is, in the minds of people there, intimately connected to the community at large. The project is their story.

> I am very excited, I am optimistic. I think the future looks fantastic, and I made that point in my address at the graduation. I told the graduates that they are very lucky — that the world is changing very fast but [our community] is also changing. Aboriginal people are making very big strides all over the world. Societies in general have accepted that you cannot pull down people for ever — making them to be on the welfare line and dependent on you all the time. They have to learn to be self-supporting and contributing members of the society. So, I am very excited about the future of the native people with regard to education — how fast we are educating our people, and the success stories out there. A lot of our educated people are coming back, and the community will prosper. (Aboriginal district administrator)

There will be many practical difficulties in finding or developing coherence where it is not now apparent. The obstacles to strategic decision making — vague, unstated or conflicting ends, idiosyncratic and uncertain means, a context that is more likely to hinder than help innovation, limited imagination, the difficulties in building a political community — will also interfere with any attempt to use projects strategically.

As great as the practical difficulties will be, the political and intellectual dimensions of the task are likely to be greater. Keeping projects from being piecemeal, and 'only' projects, will mean creating a framework that integrates education and social change and that offers people in school systems a clearer understanding of their connection to the larger whole. School systems need new conceptual and political frameworks within which their own change can occur.

Ricouer (1981) has written of 'the world of meanings in front of itself as it points to the future'. What new horizons of meaning are seen when (or if, because there is no inevitability here) pilot projects and regular practice are juxtaposed? Some of the needed changes are taking place at the edges of our systems; we need to bring these, and others like them, to the center and make of them a coherent, positive agenda for education. If activities such as these are ever to become defining, as distinct from peripheral, features of the educational systems we have, what ways of thinking about learning in educational organizations will get us from here to there?

Chapter 6

The Impact of a Changing Labor Market

Labor market change has created a major dilemma for schools. They are caught between expectations by many that schools will play a key role in labor market success for young people and the reality that their influence on labor market outcomes is relatively weak. Even where schools are able to help some students succeed, it may be at the expense of others given an overall shortage of good jobs. Solving the problem is not possible, but neither is ignoring it. It is in this framework of an intractable yet compelling problem that we describe the way the issue is understood in the school districts we have studied.

This chapter is organized in four sections — an overview of labor force change in Canada, the United States and Britain, and its implications for schools; a discussion of the way in which changes in the labor market are understood in school districts; the responses the districts are making to this issue; and a final section of issues and implications.

The Changing Labor Market and Its Implications for Schools

Much is made by governments and the media of the increased educational and skill requirements of labor force change. Indeed this is one of the prime reasons given for many educational reforms. Many government and non-governmental reports, for example argue that nations will require more education in order to remain prosperous. The argument for more education as the key to economic growth is widely accepted. A good example is provided by this excerpt from a report on education by the OECD.

> Only a well-trained and highly adaptable labour force can provide the capacity to adjust to structural change and seize new employment opportunities created by technological progress. Achieving this will in many cases entail a re-examination, perhaps radical, of the economic treatment of human resources and education. (OECD, 1993, p. 9)

The issue, however, is not so simple. For one thing, changes in education will have effect on the labor force only very slowly (Osberg, Wien and Grude, 1995). Even if dramatic improvements in learning outcomes were to occur immediately, it would be many years — perhaps decades — before students with at least a few years' experience in the improved schools actually had much impact on workplaces.

In fact, there is considerable evidence in all three countries that the work situation, especially for young people, has deteriorated markedly in the past ten or fifteen years, with rising levels of unemployment, falling real wages, and a large number of low-skill, low-wage, no-benefit, part-time jobs (Levin, 1995b; Ashton and Lowe, 1991). In all three countries manufacturing has declined in importance as an employment sector. In Britain, the reasonably well-paying industrial jobs that used to be available to 16-year-old school leavers with no further education have vanished (Roberts, 1995). In Canada and the US the decline has been somewhat less precipitous but still significant. In most countries growth in jobs over the last decade has been in services. Although some services jobs do require high skills and offer good wages and benefits, more are low skill jobs with poor pay, low job security, and few benefits (Bracey, 1996). These effects are exacerbated for many because of labor market discrimination on the basis of race and gender; evidence from several countries, for example, shows that men continue to have more access to on-the-job training than do women (Gunderson, Muszynski and Keck, 1990). It is also important to recognize that labor markets are not simply national; important differences from region to region affect the prospects of young people especially — for example, the high unemployment rates in the north of England or in Aboriginal communities in Canada and the US. Add to this picture cuts in social security benefits available to young people and eroding minimum wages (where they exist at all).

Nor is it clear that modern economies are actually requiring much higher numbers of educated workers. The most careful analyses suggest that if skill requirements in the economy are increasing, the rate of increase is slower than the rise in education levels (Berryman, 1992; Levin, 1995b). Labor market dislocations and shifts, such as growth or decline of particular industries or occupations, are more significant in their impact on the workforce than any overall trend to higher skill levels, which happens only slowly. On the whole those with more education are more successful in the labor market, although analysts argue over whether this is because of education, because education credentials serve as a filter that gives access to jobs irrespective of actual skill or knowledge, or because education is a proxy for social class so that those who are advantaged to begin with also get more education.

Levels of educational attainment have been rising in most countries. So, although the populations in Canada, the US and Britain are more educated than ever before, there are rising levels of unemployment and underemployment among those with advanced education. Significant numbers of people with post-secondary education report that their educational skills are not used in their work. The oft-advanced view that workplaces are requiring more and more advanced skills is by no means completely consistent with the evidence. The rhetoric of high skills may disguise economic strategies that actually reduce the demand for skilled labour (Bailey, 1991; Berryman, 1992).

It is also evident that the transition from school to work has changed dramatically. Schools and post-secondary institutions are still largely organized on the basis that students attend full-time, and then leave to pursue work or further education. But most young people now work a significant amount well before they finish school, even in Britain where part-time work during schooling used to be rare. Movement back and forth from education to work to education continues for many years for large numbers of people. People may cobble together some part-time work with some part-time study since they are unable either to find full-time employment or to be able to afford full-time schooling. Many young people have a difficult time obtaining a secure place in the labor market, and their plans may change frequently.

These changes pose very difficult challenges for schools. Although most educators see preparation for work as only one goal of schooling (and not the most important one at that), students tend to see the purpose of secondary school as being to prepare them to get a job (Ashton and Maguire, 1987; Rudduck, Chaplain and Wallace, 1996). The political rhetoric points, however unfairly, to schools as culprits in economic decline. Yet the evidence suggests not only that the job situation for young people is worsening, but that schools have relatively little influence on the eventual labor market outcomes of students. Schools do not control the number or kinds of jobs created in the economy, or the skill requirements of those jobs, or the hiring practices of employers. Schooling outcomes are actually less discriminatory than labor market practices (Roberts, 1995; Levin, 1995b). However the completion of secondary education — the end of the public schools' mandate and once a valued educational credential — has become a much less important labor market qualification. Other social trends such as high levels of child poverty also make it more difficult for schools to develop adequate skill levels in all children.

All three countries have also had a difficult history in regard to technical or vocational training, with the emphasis in all three having rested for many years on university education for the most able, most motivated and best connected. None of the countries has developed the sort of high quality and widely accepted technical training systems that one finds in some European countries, for example (Grubb, 1996). (Though neither has Japan, so one cannot jump to the conclusion that more technical training is some sort of educational panacea.) Efforts to develop more vocational schooling have foundered on perceptions, both inside and outside the schools, that such programs were only for those who didn't have the skills for 'the real thing' — traditional academic work.

Insofar as finishing high school has less impact than it used to on labor market outcomes, schools can expect serious problems of motivation for students. If the traditional promise of schooling — Stay in School and Get a Job — fails, it seems likely that it will be increasingly difficult to control students and to keep them interested for extrinsic reasons. Given the history especially of secondary schooling, the potential problem is very great indeed.

In the next section we describe the way our colleagues understood issues of labor market change.

Understandings of the Changing Labor Market

Across all the districts respondents did agree that the labor market was changing in many ways. These changes were generally seen as making things more difficult for young people.

> . . . economic change is really [changing] the nature of industry itself. It is difficult to predict what someone in grade 1 today will be walking into after sixteen years of schooling . . . We have to train youngsters to have a more global view than they used to. In the past the students would come out of school, and go into the community. Now many of them will come out of school and move into the global economy. (Urban district school board member)

> Years ago jobs were readily available. You could work in the railways or wherever. However, things have changed. Now there is concern in parents' minds about what their children would do even after graduation from university. That is a big concern, and we need to try to bridge that gap, and find some positions for them. We need to help students with their interests and guide them to where they can fit in. (Suburban-rural district school board member)

Our colleagues were highly aware that the expectations about work of both students and their parents were changing.

> I think all high school teachers are sensitive to the fact that they are teaching youngsters who may never work. In high schools, especially, there is a high level of sensitivity that the economic system has changed the map of school function. (Urban district school board member)

> Many of them [students] are starting to accept the fact that maybe their standard of living and the kind of work that they are going to be doing is much, much different than their parents and the opportunities are not going to be as great. (Suburban district school administrator)

Respondents to our survey of school board chairs and superintendents had similar views, with large majorities agreeing that 'young people today face more job changes and less job security' (99 percent strongly agree or agree) and that 'there are fewer jobs for high school graduates today' (80 percent agree). Labor market change was also seen as important by survey respondents, with 64 percent rating it as an important issue in their district. The mean rating for this issue, 2.5 on a 5 point scale from very important to unimportant, fell between changes in information technology (mean of 1.6) but above child poverty (mean of 3.2). Seventy percent of survey respondents described changes in work as being an important part of their own personal work, compared with 81 percent for technology and 31 percent for poverty.

District Context

The precise ways in which labor market change was seen depended in part on the context of the district. Colleagues drew our attention to the different ways in which these issues were relevant in their own settings, such as an inner-city school.

> For a number of students in the Inner City school does not necessarily lead to employment and is not necessarily perceived as leading to work. I think we need to make the tie between education and employment a stronger one. For example, we need to develop more partnerships between school and industry so that students can see that relationship. I would certainly be in favor of any programs that would tie work directly with school. (Urban district school administrator)

Especially in the suburban/rural and rural districts, we found quite a bit of pride in the accomplishments of the schools.

> No, there are not pressures [to change]. People feel that the district is providing a lot of people with opportunities, including adults. (Suburban-rural district school board member)

> We have done a study in the last three years on our graduating class to find out the number going on to post-secondary education, and the lowest we found is 86 percent. We did a follow-up on that and discovered that the 14 percent that stay behind do so basically because they are involved in a farm operation of some sort . . . (Rural district administrator)

> [Our students] have done very well right across the province. A lot of them come back here and are taking over businesses. Because of the agricultural nature of the area and the make-up of the community, many of them take an agricultural degree or program, and come back and take over the farm or a portion of the farm. (Rural district administrator)

However in a rural and agricultural setting the reality is that many young people will leave the community to obtain work, which presents its own set of challenges to the school. The school may be proud of how many of its students go on to post-secondary education, but this means that they leave the community.

> Our biggest export is our kids. There aren't the jobs for them here. If they go to university they might be able to come back to teach, but that's pretty risky, or as a doctor, and that's riskier yet.

Question Do you prepare kids for those transitions?
If we do, we don't prepare them well. We have a home/school liaison worker who tries to prepare Grade 12 kids who are going to university or technical school about where they are going to live, how much money they are going to need, and that kind of thing. That same kind of guidance isn't provided to the kids who are not going the university/technical school route. It seems to me, though, that that needs to be done, but I'm not sure that the school is the place that should be done. The school doesn't have the resources to provide that kind of preparation. (Rural district school administrator)

In the Aboriginal district, where historically very few students have even finished high school, the issue was again defined rather differently. The traditional academic program is seen to be irrelevant to many students, but the lack of paid employment on the reserve means that more educated young people will leave.

> No, I don't think our kids are ready. Due to our limited space and our limited academic program, the kids are having a lot of problems not only in the labor market but also when they want to continue their education after graduation here. They are not prepared enough to go to the university. (Aboriginal district school board member)

> Our graduates go on for more education. They understand that they have to go on with their studies. Right now there are no jobs in the community, so they cannot stay, they have to keep on, go to college. The ones that drop out have to stay. Sometimes our graduates come back. (Aboriginal district school board member)

Despite these differences, our overall view is that the context of the district did not seem to influence respondents' perceptions of the labor market as much as might have been expected. Rural respondents realized that many students would leave their community to find work and those in the Aboriginal community were well aware of the very limited economic prospects there. But little was said about the differing prospects for different streams of students or in different parts of each community, which is somewhat surprising given the local or regional (rather than provincial or national) nature of the

Canadian labor market. As we will see later, differences in context were not particularly reflected in different policies or practices around this issue.

Sources of Knowledge About Labor Market Change

Some colleagues had thought quite a bit about the import of labor market change.

> . . . for schools in general, I see global and national forces first of all. As the world has changed in terms of becoming much smaller and as trade barriers have dropped in a number of countries, we have seen the global economy change its expectation of the workers it needs and the way the world community does business. That is a definite pressure that I see working its way down to the public schools. We see it nationally in the fact that more and more of the people that the system is educating, whether at the high school level, the community college level or the university level are finding themselves without employment. (Suburban district school administrator)

> . . . the whole workforce is changing, the kind of skills that our students need are different, maybe a little more nebulous. They need written and verbal communication skills, they need to be able to work effectively with groups of people, they need to be flexible, they will probably not go into one profession or job for a lifetime, they will probably change many times. Somehow our programming and the skills we are giving those students need to reflect that . . . The whole changing workforce, the expectations and what is going to be available is going have a definite impact on our system and how we are delivering that program. (Suburban district school board member)

For the most part, however, our colleagues' views were framed in general terms. On the whole responses to questions on this subject were brief, and we heard only a few mentions of specific data regarding work opportunities, or about students' experiences with work either during or after school. Though several colleagues did comment on graduation and dropout rates in their school or district, the districts appear to have relatively little information about the experiences of current or former students in regard to work. One district mentioned a survey of graduates and another had been planning a survey for some time but not done it. Other districts or schools may survey graduates (and non-graduates), but if so this did not come up in our interviews suggesting that these data do not play a prominent role in affecting people's thinking about the issues.

In the survey we asked school board chairs and superintendents to rank their main sources of information about changes in work. From a list of eight choices (staff, students, employers, parents, data gathered by their organization, research studies from elsewhere, direct community involvements and the media), no one source appeared particularly important. Employers were ranked first and parents last, but the differences were small. The interview data suggest that such data tend to be informal — for example, through contacts with individual employers rather than through surveys. Many colleagues spoke in the interviews about partnerships with employers (more about this in the next section), but again few indicated that these partnerships had changed their ideas about the relationship of school to work.

Our colleagues said that their sense of labor market change came mainly from students and parents. Schools felt pressure from parents to prepare students for a changing future.

> I get a number of parents who have not made up their mind but who will come into my office and choose French because they want a job guarantee for their son or daughter. They see French as one edge. The whole idea of the job market is prevalent in decisions about the selection of schools and tracking for their children . . . (Urban district school administrator)

> I think there are greater expectations. People are looking to the schools to meet a lot of not only educational needs but social needs. I think that generally the community and parents are fearful about whether we are preparing the students in the best way that we can. This is probably because there is a lot of uncertainty out there about the future. What kind of a job market are they going to be facing? (Suburban district school board member)

> In the past many parents believed it was important that their children go to university. Now it is becoming obvious that the university is not the only way to get training and to earn a living. (Suburban-rural district school board member)

Students' responses to changes in work were described in different ways, with some colleagues feeling that students were becoming less motivated, and others seeing greater motivation because of more competition for jobs. Survey respondents also saw student responses varying. Sixty-one percent agreed that 'some students feel pessimistic about their future and are less motivated to complete school', but 72 percent agreed that 'some students are intensely focused on preparing for a job and are more motivated to complete school'. Of course it is quite possible that students exhibit both of these responses.

> Students in high school today have different interests. There are those who want to pursue the academics because they see the long-range professional entry as being important to them, but that is a very small group. There is another group that wants to make a dollar, with no long range plans. (Urban district administrator)

I went into a grade six class and they were talking about someone . . . who is working for $500 a month. A big argument ensued among the kids about whether or not this fellow should rather opt to collect welfare because he could get more money that way. This is at grade 6. We are a rural community, we have a lot of people who believe in a work ethic and a lot of people who are hard workers, and this was a major discussion. A lot of them were firmly convinced that welfare is the way to go on the basis of the higher income and not having to work. If one can get paid for doing nothing, they saw it as stupid to work. (Rural district school administrator)

It is sad, though, to see some of the kids that have completed their Grade 12 and are just withering away at home because there are no jobs for them here . . . [students] look around and say, maybe not consciously but subconsciously: 'What am I going to do with Grade 12 anyway? I don't want to leave the community; I know that a lot of people who have left the community have not met with success, have ended up in bad situations; I want to stay in the community. I don't need a Grade 12 degree to stay in the community.' (Aboriginal district school board member)

It is perhaps surprising that few of our colleagues spoke about students' part-time work, even though a majority of high school students have part-time jobs. Here is a potentially rich source of information about students' experience in the labor force that would help schools understand this issue. But instead of tapping students' knowledge, many educators see students' part-time work as primarily an interference with their academic tasks. One colleague in a school not involved in this study pointed out that the same students who were given responsibility for sales, cash, store security, customer relations and other tasks while at work were then required to get a pass to walk in the halls when they came to school. No wonder, she said, that they liked having a part-time job.

We also infer from these various responses that there is relatively little discussion of these issues in a structured way in the school districts. If there were we believe there would either be more consensus or more sharply etched disagreements. None of our respondents suggested that their district was spending significant time or energy on analysing issues of school and work, though many report undertaking program activities in this area (see below). The changing job situation seems to be largely an unexamined background to the work of the school districts.

The Meaning of Labor Force Change for Schools

Respondents were of different views in regard to the implications of labor market change for schools. Some saw the situation as threatening the legitimacy of schooling insofar as students may see less point to school if they think that more schooling does not lead to good employment. Some felt that schools needed to do much more to prepare students for work, while others felt there was relatively little the schools could do. A number of respondents were unsure as to which of these perspectives was best. Educators, like parents and students, know there is change but are not sure what the change means or how they might best respond to it.

One oft-expressed view was that schools were too focused on preparation for university, even though most students did not pursue this route directly from high schools (though few cited data from their own schools on these points, referring instead to figures for the school system as a whole). However our colleagues' comments here seemed inconsistent with pressures from parents as noted earlier.

> We've known for some time that 22 or 26 percent of the kids are going off to university and there's no guarantee that they will have the kinds of jobs that used to exist. We're worried about what are we doing for the other 75 percent. As a result we're looking at what is it we are teaching and asking are we providing them with the links to the real world? (Urban district administrator)

> We don't have the facilities for vocational training, and some of these children, because of their attendance problems have low academic grades, and then they get frustrated and just quit. Our other option would have been to gear them to vocational trades like plumbing or electrical but we don't have those programs here. (Aboriginal district school board member)

Some wondered whether the frequent rhetoric about business needs accurately represented the reality facing young people.

> Generally speaking I'd say that our own staff is out of date in terms of knowing what businesses want. I don't even know if business know what they want. I've been to business education conferences and I hear people from business say one thing, and then I read in the paper that businesses . . . are having to lay off members of their staff, so it makes me wonder if businesses have a good sense of what they are about. (Urban district administrator)

> When we talk with people from large business, they say they want people with good social skills, communication skills, problem solving and cooperation skills. When we talk to people from small business, they are saying that they want people with specific employable skills. Then there is a group of people who want to go back to the basics . . . We can not cater to all these goals because they are not compatible. (Suburban district administrator)

Other colleagues expressed strong beliefs that the school should continue to focus on general education, and that preparation for work could not and should not become the main purpose of schools. They thought that as more education was required for jobs, there would be more pressure on students to complete secondary school or to meet post-secondary entrance requirements.

> My view is that it's not the technology, it's not the content of the study but it's to develop a loving, caring human being and that all these other things are tools by which a person can gain a sense of accomplishment and therefore build self esteem. I'm not interested in having a bright chemist blow up the world. (Suburban district administrator)

> I think our schools are training our students more to go into university than they are training students to go into the workplace. My beliefs are that I would rather see them continue to train students to go on to university or community colleges because if they are pushed in that direction and decide to drop out while they are enrolled in university or college, they are better off than if they had dropped out in high school. They are more likely to be able to succeed. (Rural district school board member)

Survey respondents were asked about the skills they thought students needed to obtain work. By large margins they favored general and personal skills over traditional vocational skills. For example, more than 90 percent rated critical thinking skills, interpersonal skills and positive attitudes to work as very important, while only 56 percent gave the same importance to specific job skills and 69 percent to work experience.

Whatever their views on these issues, our colleagues recognized that the nature and purpose of schooling were being called into question by changes in work.

> . . . where are all the kids going to be employed after graduation? I think this is a major challenge. We have to ensure that the skills we provide our kids with are going to be marketable. We face a major dilemma in terms of our general high school program which equips the kids well for nothing. If kids have got specific skills in vocational areas, they would be quite marketable on graduation. We often think that if students do well in [academic] programs, then they can go on to university, but even for that group I have concerns because we are not even sure where a lot of the university students are to be employed after graduation. I think things have become more complicated in this regard and I see my number one concern as determining what our high school programs should equip the kids for. (Suburban district school administrator)

It is important to change our thinking that education alone is the answer. Being well educated without a job does not do a lot for your feelings about yourself or anything else. It is important for us to relate to the job market. (Rural district school board member)

We turn next to what our colleagues told us about their responses to labor market change.

Responding to a Changing Labor Market

At the most basic level, our colleagues had divided views as to how well the schools were coping with the impact of labor market change. Seventy-three percent of survey respondents rated preparing students for work as important or very important for the schools, but only 11 percent rated schools as doing very well in this area, with another 47 percent giving a rating of 'good'.

Among colleagues we interviewed, a minority felt that the response had been quite good.

There's a greater emphasis on skill now and, in general, there's a whole different outlook. Even at the elementary level there is an awareness that priorities have changed . . . You have to expect this kind of sensitivity. Television, radio, newspapers, all speak about the changes to the economic system. (Urban district school board member)

Most expressed the view that schools had not done enough to meet the challenges of changes in work.

There are some general notions about how we can work, but we are not geared up as a school district to respond to this issue. (Urban district administrator)

Most kids need some kind of connection with the outside world and that school really has some connection and application to the outside world. Schools do a poor job of this. Kids don't see the connection, and in some cases I think it would be difficult to demonstrate a connection . . . It's important to make more connections like that. We've had a number of discussions on this issue within the district . . . and the efforts that would have to be made to set something like this up would be unbelievable. (Rural district school administrator)

Despite this self-criticism, respondents mentioned a number of strategies that were being used in their districts to try to improve linkages between school and work. Respondents tended to mention the same basic strategies in all the districts. Some strategies that we know to be present in at least some of the districts — for example, gender equity projects in science and mathematics — did not come up in our interviews.

Most frequently mentioned was the development of partnerships of various kinds with employers and post-secondary institutions. These are occurring at all levels of the school system and take a variety of forms. They are seen as having benefits for students, staff, and the partner organizations. The number of such partnerships appears to be growing quite rapidly. Most partnerships seem to work within the existing structures of each institution; efforts to change those roles or structures in lasting ways are not common at this point.

> ... we currently have in place a variety of committees to consult with the academic and business communities. We also focus on establishing business partnerships so that business becomes involved directly in our schools on the consultation level, and on the practical instruction level, where business experts team teach with our staff. As an example, we have a research facility in one of our high schools where experts team teach with our staff in areas like Chemistry and Physics ... We also have joint committees that look specifically at technology and how to utilize it. (Urban district administrator)

> I could see that we will have more partnerships with business. We already have a couple of those in place, but I think that we will seek to develop more liaison with the business community. The kind of programs we offer and the timing of those may have to be more flexible as we have students who, for economic reasons, have to go out to work and go to school at the same time. (Suburban district school board member)

> The district has made connections with different faculties in a variety of [post-secondary] institutions ... We are establishing working relationships with these institutions. (Suburban-rural district school board member)

A second strategy concerns professional development for staff. Many respondents recognize that teachers are not necessarily well-equipped to deal with issues of work since many of them have limited experience outside the school system. However this strategy appears to be more an idea than a reality at this point; few respondents talked about specific measures to change teachers' skills and knowledge — not surprising, perhaps, given recent cuts in budgets for professional development activities in many jurisdictions.

> I think the teachers need to know more about the real world, what goes on outside education. All of us get entrenched in the world we are in, and I think we all need to look beyond and have some experience outside. We need work experience for teachers, not just kids.

We need to listen to people who work in other environments. We are not preparing kids to be teachers. This does not mean we should shut down the system. (Suburban district administrator)

Simply having caring, interested staff is seen as an important measure in itself.

I think one thing that is really important is having people on staff, particularly, although not exclusively, in the high school who aren't there just to teach their particular subject area but are keeping their finger on the pulse of what is happening as far as careers go, because I think everyone in the high school has to be acting as a sort of un-official guidance counsellor. (Aboriginal district school administrator)

A third often-mentioned strategy was improving guidance services and information to students to help them make better choices about education and work.

. . . through our programs some of our grade 5 and 6 children go to [a business] on a regular basis and work on integrated projects . . . These young students are seeing the working world and the people in the business are seeing our inner-city students as people who can work there when they leave school. (Urban district administrator)

Recently our grade 9 students attended a career symposium . . . They learned what the educational requirements are for the various pro-fessions. About 80 percent of the kids thought it was great, about 20 percent could have stayed back. It helps them to be aware of what is out there and what they require to pursue their goals and making sure they know they should not cut off their opportunities. (Suburban-rural district school administrator)

The evidence suggests, however, that though school guidance and infor-mation services may have other uses, they have relatively little impact on students' labor market choices or outcomes (Rudduck *et al.*, 1996). Family remains a much more powerful influence on students' plans than any informa-tion the school might provide.

Co-operative education, mentoring and entrepreneurship programs were described as valuable programs, though they were often focused on students who were not seen as capable of regular academic work.

We are now looking at co-op education in which we can send the students out on job shadowing types of things. I have been involved in preparing students for the workforce through these programs. I think that we still do not do enough in preparing the average and lower student for job expectations. (Rural district administrator)

. . . there has to be a stream for the students who want to stay here and need different kinds of skills to do that. And perhaps more emphasis on entrepreneurship because this is a community of 3,000 people. There is an opportunity here for somebody who wants to run a small business but you need to have the training to do that. (Aboriginal district school administrator)

A fourth vehicle mentioned by our colleagues was increased use of technology. A number of them saw computer use particularly as a new requisite for jobs, and commented on steps being taken to ensure students had some experience working with computers. This issue is developed more fully in Chapter 7.

There is rapid advancement in computer technology. Computer systems and languages are changing so rapidly, and the use of technology by industries has advanced very quickly. So, again we must attempt to keep up with the changes. (Urban district administrator)

I have a lot of hopes for what can be done with computers but I do not know a lot about them myself. I think the students should be given a basic idea of how to learn using almost anything and then they could learn to do the required programs later. I do not think that anyone else here would agree with that. (Rural district school board member)

For some, as mentioned earlier, a good general education remains the best preparation for work.

I suppose the best answer an educator comes up with is that you try to inculcate in them a desire and an ability to learn . . . I guess you take natural interests and abilities and develop them so that hopefully they'll be life long learners. (Urban district administrator)

It is not possible now to base your courses strictly on content. This is because of the computerization of everything and the huge amount of new information that is coming out all the time. What you really have to prepare students to do is to be able to think critically, to go out and find information when they need it to answer their own questions in a critical way, and to analyze information. The amount of information people have to deal with now is just enormous. It doesn't really matter what profession you choose to go into, you are going to be in a situation where what you learned in school is going to be out of date in a year, so you have got to have better thinking skills. (Aboriginal district school administrator)

We also note that four of the participating districts have schools with extensive vocational programs. These programs weren't mentioned by all our colleagues but the existence of the schools was a basic element of their approach to preparing students for work, providing an alternative model for students who were not succeeding in the academic program. As was noted earlier in the chapter, though, and as several colleagues mentioned in their comments, vocational education has never attained anything like parity of esteem with the more traditional academic program. There is good reason for this preference; the evidence continues to indicate (Roberts, 1995; Grubb, 1996) that academic education produces better long-term employment outcomes than do vocational programs. Despite all the talk about the value and honor of craft and technical skills, students and parents are quite aware of what carries currency in the larger society.

Despite the expressed concerns about current practices, we heard only a few mentions of more fundamental changes being considered. New models such as career academies are only beginning to be discussed.

> One of the [issues] that we are looking at right now that I think is going to be ongoing is questions of restructuring, particularly at the high school level . . . I think that we have done a really good job of changing with the times and coming out with some fairly innovative ideas, innovative programming and program delivery at the primary, elementary and perhaps even into Junior High. Our sense is that maybe we have not been as progressive as we would like to be at the high school level. We recognize that probably the greatest percentage of our students are not going to go on to the university level. They are going to be looking at something different and we are really wondering whether or not we are meeting the needs of those students. Over the next few years we will be looking at how that programming is delivered. Getting away from some of the standard blocks of time that we might deliver a class and encouraging more integration of teaching at the high school level. That is probably going to be one of the biggest initiatives over the next few years. (Suburban district school board member)

In this case we can note that more than two years after this interview, the district is still studying changes in high schools and no restructuring has yet occurred.

In the surveys we asked school board chairs and superintendents to comment on a range of possible strategies schools might employ to address changes in work facing students. Table 6.1 summarizes the percent of respondents identifying each strategy as effective, and the percent indicating that their school district was using this strategy.

Several points about these responses are striking. First, nine of the eleven strategies were rated as potentially effective by 70 percent or more of our respondents, suggesting that the districts have a wide range of potential approaches to use. Even more significant are the very large gaps between perceptions of the effectiveness of these practices and reports of their actual use.

Table 6.1: Strategies for dealing with labor market change

Strategy	Effective	Implemented
Place greater emphasis on attributes such as punctuality or initiative	93	41
Teach more explicitly about the labor market and finding work	88	22
Develop collaborative programs with employers and unions	88	54
Provide more work experience or similar	86	62
Develop collaborative programs with post-secondary institutions	81	25
Strengthen teaching of basic skills	79	64
Strengthen guidance counselling	74	51
Teach entrepreneurship	74	24
Provide more specific skills training	72	47
Have more testing of students' career interests	57	30
Reduce tracking and streaming	36	24

Note: Percent of survey respondents

Only four of the eleven strategies are reported as being used by even half the respondents (and two of these by a bare majority), suggesting that current approaches were not based on a strategic analysis of what might be most effective.

The practices that were mentioned are seen to operate within the confines of the existing structure of schooling. They are add-on or substitute programs rather than changes in the basic operation of the schools. Two are completely consistent with existing school practices — more guidance counselling and better teaching of basic skills — and two others — work experiences and partnerships — that are overlays on the traditional school program. We did not see very much evidence that any of the districts were thinking about larger-scale changes that might be necessary given changes in the labor market and the lives of their students. For example, although many respondents talked about the need to move away from an emphasis on university preparation, we heard no examples of steps being taken to do so except for particular kinds of students, for whom program options, though they are often viewed as inferior, have long been available. No respondents mentioned having a district strategy in place on this issue. None of the districts appears to have made this issue a priority. Labor force change is seen as a big problem, but there are no 'big' answers.

Barriers to Responding

We also asked survey respondents to assess the barriers to greater action on this issue in their school or district. Table 5.2 gives fuller data on this item. In the case of changes in work, respondents rated two barriers as most important (lowest on the 5 point scale). These were lack of support from the provincial government (mean of 2.5) and lack of resources (mean of 2.9). In other words, respondents felt that the most important barriers to doing better in this area lay outside their jurisdiction. They accepted the issue as an important one, but blamed senior government and lack of resources for any weaknesses in approach.

> We need to be able to answer 'What is the function of education within that and what do we need to do to attain our goals?' We do not seem to have any of that from any one. When our provincial ministers combine direction with their federal counterparts, nothing comes out of it, there is no direction. They produce one report after another, only to have it dismissed or not implemented. (Rural district school administrator)

> All we can do, I think, is discuss like this and formulate ideas, try to put them into some vision, and share them with people, hoping that somebody with some power somewhere is listening. (Urban district school administrator)

Conclusion: Schools in a Changing Labor Market

Schools cannot solve labor market problems for students, and the evidence reviewed earlier suggests that schools have less influence on labor market outcomes than used to be the case. Our colleagues are certainly aware that labor market changes have implications for their students and for their organizations. But action seems largely disassociated from analysis of the problem. More study of international, national and local evidence on the changing nature of work and the actual outcomes of students might help schools work through what is most useful to do. This is an issue that needs more discussion both among educators and among students and parents. Evidence is that students are much more focused on school as preparation for work than are teachers (Goodlad, 1984; Ashton and Maguire, 1987; Cullingford, 1990). Parents are in-between. These different expectations and their implications for schools need to be raised and debated among all parties.

Our data also suggest that schools have focused on a relatively small number of strategies in improving their link to work. The strategies being used seem reasonable ones, but there are many other possibilities that might be explored. These could include building the study of work into existing courses, drawing in people with wider experience in the labor force, creating more opportunities for staff to work in non-school settings, running school programs in workplaces or workplaces in the school, operating joint programs with employers, unions, or post-secondary institutions, expanding opportunities for students to study part time and work part time, and making students' ongoing work an area of study. Some of the new developments in other countries, such as employer-led training or career academies also seem promising.

To a considerable extent educators maintain a bifurcation between general education and education for work. Though many of our colleagues talked about the excessive importance attached to preparation for university, there is little sign of that changing; in fact, pressures from students and parents may be pushing towards a more academic focus. Yet learning about work can be as challenging a part of a general education as can any other subject. Studying the way work is organized, labour law, collective bargaining, sales and marketing, or any number of other work-related topics could be an integral part of a strong curriculum, taught in ways that engaged students and that did not see them as cogs in an industrial machine. Since most high school students already work in some way, students' own experiences and interests could be an important part of this study.

Changes in labor markets are such that schools' traditional strategies are less and less adequate to students' needs. Schools will need to consider a strategic response to this issue that involves not only some specific programs for some selected students, but that involves changes in the overall curriculum of the school, the training and professional development of staff, the way in which the school organizes and timetables, and especially relationships with other institutions such as post-secondary education and employers. We will need to reconsider secondary school program tracks and the whole idea of vocational education.

Although our survey respondents identified outside limitations as critical to their work, it is hard to avoid the conclusion that the issue of work and its relationship to schooling has simply not received enough attention in school systems. Our colleagues see that more could be done, but has not been done. While resource limits and other pressures are very real, schools simply have not seen issues of work as a priority for limited time, energy and money.

Chapter 7

Schools Coping with the Impact of Information Technology

Information technology is widely seen as a change in society to which schools must respond, and a development that has tremendous implications for education. Yet a considerable literature documents the relatively weak impact of technology on schools over many years (Cuban, 1986; Cohen, 1988; Snider, 1992); what Cohen (1987) described as 'extravagant hopes of easy revolution . . . followed by a steep drop into dreary disappointment' (p. 154).

Explanations for this state of affairs vary, but generally relate to the lack of clarity about the potential value and best uses of technology.

> . . . schools used television and radio as a mere medium, a mere instrument, denying it the right to teach in its own way . . . No effort was made to adapt teaching methods or to use the instrument imaginatively . . . the media were expected to do everything, both what schools could not do and what they no longer wished to do . . . In such cases it was no longer school on television, it was television acting as school and taking its place. (Balle, 1991, p. 104)

> The primary reason technology has failed to live up to its promise lies in the fact that it has been viewed as an answer to the wrong question. Decisions about technology purchases and uses are typically driven by the question of how to improve the effectiveness of what schools are already doing — not how to transform what schools do . . . Moreover, as has been typical with innovations of the past, scant attention has been paid to preparing teachers and administrators to use new technology well and even less to their preferences about hardware and software. (David, 1992, p. 3)

We note that in the analysis that follows, information technology was taken by most of our colleagues to be largely equivalent to computers and related devices such as CD-ROM and Internet access, a view that has been criticized as diverting attention from broader concepts of technology. In the remainder of the chapter we adopt our colleagues' usage of 'information technology' and 'computer technology' as interchangeable. We also remind the reader that the views expressed came from administrators and elected officials, not from classroom teachers.

With the exception of one or two people, everyone we interviewed or surveyed assumed that schools needed to purchase and use computers, and to ensure that students had experience working with these machines. The commitment to using information technology, however, did not arise out of processes of planning or analysis, and was weakly linked to concepts of teaching and learning. Instead, technology use was a process driven by volunteer teachers and administrators inside schools, and parents, community groups and employer organizations outside schools. Financial, administrative and political issues appear to have dominated the agenda at the senior level, and debates over costs were central.

Over the last ten years the school districts have invested a lot of time, energy and money in computer technology and the in-service education of teachers, and the number of classrooms and curricular areas in which computers are used is growing. Still, it seems that information technology is at best an adjunct to education, not yet integrated into people's thinking about teaching and learning. Some of the educators in our study expressed a sense of the educational potential of information technology, but few indicated that they have begun to explore that potential more fully.

The developments that have occurred took place within a largely unexamined view of what schooling is about and how it should be conducted. Much depends on what individuals happen to have heard, seen, or read, and most of the attention is given to what other schools or school systems are doing. The districts had not organized a discussion of the broader meaning of technology. Although some of our colleagues spoke about the potential of technology to individualize learning and give students greater autonomy, districts do not seem to be pursuing these possibilities in any systematic way. Technology may or may not end up reshaping schooling, but it is surely important to put that question on the agenda in a direct way.

The experience of our colleagues shows that it takes time for technology to be accommodated to existing practice, and even longer for existing practice to change so as to take advantage of the new potential of the technology. Neither will happen without real effort. In organizations, developing new ways of working is both an individual and collective process, shaped not just by various demands and supports but also by organizational culture and the meanings which people develop around technology and its use in education.

From an organizational learning point of view, the question of technological change is interesting in at least two respects. First, literature on organizational learning tends not to pay enough attention to time: our data suggest this is a crucial dimension, with development taking a decade or more. Second, the literature suggests organizational learning is a convergent process with some definite outcomes, whereas our data suggest that the outcomes of technological change can be divergent, with change opening a widening array of possibilities rather than creating one new way of doing things.

A Modal Story

Our conversations about social change usually (the Aboriginal school district was an exception, and so the data to follow do not include them) turned to technology. Because the districts seemed in respect to technology to be much more alike than different, we have chosen to collapse their four stories into our one. The following narrative is our reconstruction of their experience and is intended as a bridge to analysis. The form of the narrative suggests that learning about and responding to technological change takes time and involves many complex, diverse and uncertain organizational processes. We explore these later in this chapter.

The implementation of computer technology has been a high priority for the districts and their administrators.

One of our board priorities is the whole area of technology. Last year our budget reflected that in that we put significant dollars into acquisitions that were going to improve our technology programming. Now, when we are looking at building new schools one of the key areas that we are thinking about is, 'Are we providing the hardware and the where-with-all within that school to get onto electronic highways?' It is something that is very visible within the district. (Suburban district school board member)

Pressure from parents, community groups and students was an important impetus for bringing computers into schools.

The community looks upon the programs favorably and they don't want to see them cut. If it meant that their tax rates would have to increase to maintain those programs, they would probably look upon that favorably as well. (Rural district administrator)

In our discussions with the community, the Chamber of Commerce, the service groups, the individuals who come in representing companies to talk about scholarships, bursaries and curriculum, and from our own teachers going on field trips where computers are now taken for granted we have come to see computers as being a requirement for any of our graduates if they plan to be competitive in the work field. That is almost as much of a given as being knowledgeable in math or language arts. (Suburban-rural district school adminstrator)

Pressures aside, many people believed the economic case for technology is strong.

[T]he reality existing in the work world and the world of tomorrow is that without a knowledge, understanding and an awareness of technology, our kids cannot survive. It does have a direct impact on what we do. We are catching up with the kids. (Suburban district school administrator)

There was some debate about the educational merits of information technology. Proponents claimed:

We are in the middle of an information explosion. We are attempting to channel our energies towards promoting life-long learning and awareness. To me this is a fundamental change from when I started. We have shifted from the mere acquisition of content knowledge to the realization of the importance of technology and what impact that will have on the life of kids. (Suburban district school administrator)

But a number of people had reservations.

It is always a problem to me because I ask whether computers are really the crux of education. Yes, there are a lot of things that one can learn from television and videos but justifying the expenditures seems horrendous sometimes . . . Sometimes I wonder if we could do without it and as soon as students graduate from high school they could take a course in computers rather than having them all through school. (Rural district school board member)

Resources for hardware and in-service education were a constraint and a source of frustration.

I find it a frustrating aspect because I do not feel that we have been able to take full advantage of computers due to cost. We think that it would be really helpful if we could have a certain subject taught in a classroom and take advantage of distance education. Yet the information we have is that it is really too expensive for us to do it. (Rural district school board member)

It is easier for us to buy equipment than to train the staff. We have a surplus in our budget so the board is able to purchase equipment since it is a one-time expenditure. Where we have a problem is in the training of staff but we are doing our best within the limits of available resources. (Urban district administrator)

Obsolescence was a fear.

I find it frustrating to dump thousands of dollars down a drain because the machines are antiquated by the time they are in the schools. (Rural district school board member)

I think educators are faced with a frustration that as fast as you put them in they become obsolete, and yet you can't not put them in. The equipment that I had installed when I was a principal twelve years ago is worthless today. I don't think you can go any other way because we have to help students to become computer literate. We are committed, and continually frustrated. We can never catch up, let alone get ahead. (Urban district administrator)

And there seemed to be no educational plan concerning information technology.

The vastness of technology, however, imposes difficulties on the school system because it has been very difficult, in some way, to know where to focus. It is expensive to put the technology in place, and putting the technology in schools is not really a solution to how we should use the technology in education. (Urban district school administrator)

The developments that have occurred seem to have resulted primarily from the efforts of volunteers. Technology is perhaps the most compelling example of the project approach discussed in Chapter 5.

The start of it becomes school initiative. If a school is taking off in a technology sense, other people will become informed about it through the initiative of the Superintendent at an Admin meeting where the school is asked to share what is being done. Then the other schools, who maybe had different initiatives but not a technological one, will start coming and asking for additional or similar supports to those that were given to the school that developed the initial proposal. (Suburban district school administrator)

Highly motivated volunteers seemed better able to muster the support of the district, and this is seen to result in differences or inequities within the system.

In many of those schools there are some people who are highly motivated and highly competent in technology and there are a number of innovative programs in place in those schools. In [one school] for instance, there are four computer labs used for many things — as a subject base, as instruction assistance, for keyboarding and knowledge, and everyone is scheduled into the labs. Students coming out of [that school] will be competent in computer technology. Other schools, of course, don't have the same kind of expertise and in those schools there isn't much going on, so the situation is varied. We haven't been able to get a handle on it because of the newness of the technology. (Urban district school board member)

Most often it's where you have a key principal who believes in the program, who will find the right people, and badger for resources. (Urban district administrator)

The pace of development has been slowed by the fear of some teachers of technology.

> Teachers, especially female and older female teachers (which pretty much describes our primary staff), are scared to death of computers and technology. We need to get more young people into the schools who have hands-on experience with technology. (Rural district school administrator)

> The biggest thing we have problems with is older staff members who are uncomfortable with the computers in the classroom. The hardest thing we have had to do is to work on that. (Rural district administrator)

Some teachers also see teaching in non-technological terms.

> Most teachers are artsy fartsy social worker/Arts degree types of people and they are a community that I don't think has adopted technology. Technology is being imposed on teachers who aren't that interested in it. (Urban district school board member)

> Many of them have been successfully teaching for years without the use of computers, and now we are asking them to teach in a new and different way. Those teachers ask 'why don't I just keep teaching in a way that I know works?' (Urban district administrator)

Development seems to have occurred incrementally.

> Most schools originally introduced computers into the top end of Junior or into Senior High for accounting, database work, spread sheets and word-processing. Basically, that is where the curriculum started as well. The curriculum now recognizes computer awareness down to kindergarten but it is really antiquated and needs rewriting. It is dated in the computer world. We have been taking things from a computer awareness perspective and moving them down the ladder, out of the Senior High which is far beyond what the curriculum is suggesting and into the Grades 5–9 level. We have now taken the awareness and are introducing it at the Kindergarten level. It is not that the curriculum does not do this, but it is kind of airy-fairy and fluffy compared to the hands on approach. . . .
>   When computers first came out, they were used mainly for remediation with very little thought process and did not specifically develop students' thinking. It was only things that could be done on a piece of paper. They have gone so far beyond that now. We use the computer for reading and spelling. The computer says the word and the student then has to not only write the word, but can also bring up

a picture of the object. The key is dove-tailing it with what the teacher is doing to teach reading. We encourage teachers to incorporate the technology with what they are doing as a teacher. (Rural district administrator)

Thinking back, about ten or eleven years ago when computers first came in, we wondered how we would get them into the school system. Do we just go out and buy them, then bring them in, or do we do something else? Eventually we decided to hire a part-time co-ordinator with expertise in this area, then we got supplies of computers, and later we provided training in computer literacy. This enabled some people in each school to acquire skill in the use of computers. Workshops were organized and computer literacy was improved. Computer laboratories were provided in the schools and the process kept building up. We never discourage anybody from trying to learn how to use computers, even if it means taking the equipment home to practice with. Of course, we ensured at the board level that proper control was established to avoid misuse. In our district the computer is used as a tool in the classroom or the library or wherever it is needed. (Suburban-rural school board member)

Applications are becoming more extensive.

We have provided an Apple II GS computer for every resource room for remedial work. We are now going into the larger Macintosh computers so that the students can get a chance to use the CD ROM within the resource area. The resource area has kept the students aware of new technology such as the CD ROMs and the Macintosh and what it can offer. At the same time we offer remedial programs through the Apple II GS. (Rural district administrator)

We have one, for example, in the band room. It is a fantastic program that the band teacher and his students use to manipulate music by playing the melody, accompanying it, and doing any number of changes. We have jazz bands who write their own material so they are using the computer as well . . . We have computers in the Art room which we will be using for Graphic Arts and one in Chemistry which is used for demonstration purposes. We also use one for Physics. (Rural district principal)

Courses in various subjects are being taught with the use of the computers, rather than teaching computers as a course in and of itself. I think this is very important. For example, computers are used in English and History to do searches and to prepare homework. There are only so many people that need to know what a computer is and how it works, just as there are only so many people that need to know how to service a car. (Rural district school board member)

The educational objectives of computer technology are being clarified.

We have recently made an announcement that we feel that all of our graduates must be exposed to, and comfortable with, computers. That they know the basics of running a computer in terms of turning it on, retrieving information and knowing its capabilities. We are not saying that we expect all of our students to be computer programmers with computer science. We are expecting them to be able to come in and be able to retrieve information, to go to the library and retrieve articles. Things that show they are completely comfortable with using computers. Within three years that will be happening if it is not already. (Suburban-rural district school administrator)

And some attention is being given to changes in the role of teachers implied by technology.

[W]e have gone through some evolutions. In computer technology, for example, initially it meant that everybody was going to be a programmer, and we started teaching programming to all the teachers. Then we realized that the computer was going to be a tool, and that 'you don't have to know how to program anymore than you need to be mechanic to drive a car.' So we shifted from that but then the focus became, 'we are going to computerize all the subject areas', so it really wasn't the computer as a tool as much as computerizing everything. And all of a sudden we have moved from there to recognizing that the computer has to be a tool that enhances learning. It has to link with the curriculum but it is not to be served by the curriculum but rather a servant to the curriculum. That is really where we are right now. . . .

There is a danger, however, that we may just stay at the surface and that we are amazed by the sheer amount of knowledge, but never go in depth. This will lead to our goals being too general. That is one of the dangers we have to look at. We have to go beyond the novelty of accessibility of information and really explore how we can use the information. And, more importantly, ask: 'What information am I looking at before I even go into it, to become more efficient?' I see that as one of the big impacts. Its impact will be felt more by the staff than the students. . . .

The teacher previously was the depository of information, if not the sole one, certainly the main one. Now that is no longer the situation. The teacher is now a facilitator — not a reservoir of knowledge. Students are allowed to discover. In that respect the computer has had a significant effect on how we see teaching and learning. (Suburban district administrator)

Still, the future is a question mark.

> I still have difficulty visualizing the full impact of technology on our delivery system, because I had thought at one stage during the 1970s that the school of the future would be a drop in center and that students would be doing a lot at home. Technology would decentralize schooling so the drop in center would provide distance education. As I come to the end of my career, I am not as sure that this would be realistic or possible, mainly because of the very great need for the socializing aspect of education, cooperating and working together. (Suburban district administrator)

> In terms of technology, we're just scratching the surface. The district has struggled to try to keep up with technology. (Rural district school administrator)

People talked of three images of the future. One is teaching and learning with technology as an adjunct.

> Ultimately computers will have to be put into the classrooms to be used as a resource. (Urban district administrator)

> It is more of an adjunct. I hope so. I can't visualize technology replacing the human interaction of school. I see that interaction as being very important. (Urban district administrator)

A second image is of a change in teaching and learning.

> If we use it teachers are going to have to change their style of teaching and allow students to be turned loose on projects. That shouldn't be too far in the future, I hope. I think we're making a big mistake by trying to hold the kids in classrooms and teach them stuff. There is some stuff you need to teach them, but I think they should be taught more about systems than stuff. They can always look the stuff up. I'm not sure how that applies to Science, but I'm sure that's the case with Social Studies. (Rural district school administrator)

The third image is the technological classroom.

> We are about to connect with Internet and trying to keep abreast of everything that is happening, not only in our area but globally as well, through Internet. We will be hooked up to it this September. We have made advances in technology in areas of computer-assisted drafting. We just had a winner in a cross-Canada competition using the computer in the band program. We are involved in the general use of

technology in areas of word-processing — we have two computer labs in the high schools. We see the need for a DOS background, so the new machines we are purchasing for the high schools will be the power PC's that can flip-flop back and forth, as soon as they drop in price a little bit. (Rural district administrator)

I see there will be linkages between classrooms and school libraries, between school libraries and other systems in Internet. I see limitless kinds of learning potential and a lot more fun in learning through information technology. (Urban district administrator)

Technology and the Organizational Culture of School Systems

The experience reported in the four districts and in the surveys seems to illustrate a pattern of organizational change that, initially at least, places initiative at the parent, teacher or school principal level, with senior administrators and policy makers providing support as they are able. At the outset, some ten years ago, there were no comprehensive plans or policies regarding technology. Today, decisions about computer use continue to be made at the school and classroom level, though they are shaped by central budgets, policies regarding equity in resource allocation, and encouragement by senior administrators and policy makers. Authority and resources have become subject to central policies and procedures, though initiative in computer use remains decentralized.

In the earliest phases, senior administrators and policy makers were in a reactive position, with implementation driven by volunteers inside the system or pressure groups outside the system.

[I]t comes from kids, it comes from parents. [Parents] have lost their job as a result of technology. They are saying, 'If my kid does not have the where-with-all to survive in that kind of environment, he is dead in the water.' (Suburban district school administrator)

If, for instance, a principal attends a conference where he learns about a new piece of software, he then brings that information back and shares it with the other principals in the group. Then, to make it effective, there are innovative and creative teachers who can transform these ideas into classroom implementation. At that point teacher groups get together and exchange information. (Urban district school board member)

Eventually, pressures began to build, causing financial and political strains on the systems. Policies and coordination were necessary, partly because hardware and training are costly. With limited budgets and competing priorities this usually meant a phasing in process, such as placing technology in high schools before elementary schools or in computer laboratories before classrooms. Costs were exacerbated because computer technology has been an additional expense, not a substitute for other expenditures such as salaries, instructional materials, or library books. Only one respondent mentioned such a possibility, and did so in the context of some skepticism about information technology in education.

It seems the pace of technological change contributes to impatience, within schools as well as with them. Yet development is not just a function of hardware, but also of what is to be done with that hardware. The absence of goals and an unclear understanding of the place of computers in teaching and learning contributes significantly to the perception of obsolescence. Many now-obsolete computers are more than adequate for certain basic functions such as word processing and calculation, but this is overlooked because technological imperatives (to have the latest, fastest, most powerful computers available) overtake unclear educational objectives.

A second reason for policy and coordination was to promote equity (or at least avoid the political controversy of too much inequity) among schools.

> I think in computer technology [the school board has] indicated that in order to try to be equitable, all K to 3 schools have at least one computer in their classrooms, the 4–6 have Macs and the Junior Highs have labs. At the high school level they have also indicated a similar kind of equity. I think that is seen as a whole district. . . . [T]he personalities at the high schools are fairly strong . . . but when it comes to getting resources they want at least the same. (Suburban district administrator)

Although senior administrators and policy makers tended to see equity issues as mainly involving differences among schools, in one district it was implied that the equity question is broader than this.

> We haven't addressed the issue of allowing for excellence or schools to really develop in this area. I know some people say that this is streaming schools and we don't want that. I'm at a point where I feel that it doesn't matter what you label it, you have to offer bright students the opportunity to keep on going with their computer interests. (Urban district administrator)

Some people in the latter district might even agree with Emihovich (1990) that computer literacy is a form of cultural capital, and that patterns of technology use in schools may be related to the social background of children. She suggests that there will be differences '. . . between children who experience the

computer in terms of what it tells them to do and children who learn to view
the computer as an interactive partner' (p. 230). Drill and control applications
will be more common with disadvantaged children, and she cautions that use
only for remedial work is a form of deskilling. However, our broader study
revealed that our colleagues are very uncertain about the nature and extent of
their responsibilities to children from poor families.

District policy was also intended to develop some focus for efforts, to
rationalize the acquisition of technology and to encourage more teachers to
use computers in classrooms and school computer laboratories. All the districts
appointed computer coordinators with these tasks in mind.

Yet the overall educational focus of their efforts seemed unclear. The
systems seem committed to doing interesting things, but do not appear to have
an overall educational framework to guide their work. Little formal study of
the educational uses of information technology was reported compared with
a primary reliance on personal contacts for information; only 10 percent of the
survey respondents said that research studies done by other organizations
have been an important influence on their own knowledge of information
technology, and none reported conducting their own research. There are plans
for acquiring, distributing and networking information technology (90 percent
of the survey respondents reported having a district plan for information technology), but the plans we saw focused largely on hardware and software
configurations, with much less thought given to the educational uses of information technology.

> I remember participating in a meeting eight or nine years ago when
> we were discussing computers in the school, and I asked what are we
> doing it for? What are we trying to achieve? My feeling is that we
> didn't answer the question then, and I'm not sure if we have answered
> the question now. I think we're slow, and I'm not sure what the plan
> is. (Urban district administrator)

Most of our colleagues appear to believe that committed volunteers are
enough to drive institutional change. Over 70 percent of the survey respondents said that the development of information technology in their districts was
primarily due to the initiative of individual teachers and administrators; 87
percent believe that encouraging interested teachers to take initiatives in this
area is one of the most effective strategies for change. But there is likely to be
a continuing tension between reliance on volunteers and institutional change.
In one of the four districts there was a hint that technology and in-service
education alone will not be sufficient to drive change, and that these need to
be coupled with new institutional arrangements. Pacey (1984) observed that
innovations are '. . . the outcome of a cycle of mutual adjustments between
social, cultural and technical factors' (p. 25). It seems that the social and cultural adjustments have yet to be made.

The Portrayal of Teachers

In our interviews teachers were described as volunteers or resisters. The work of volunteers was generally supported. Teachers who have not embraced technology were termed 'resisters' in the interviews and described by 90 percent of our survey respondents as in need of substantial retraining. There was no mention of their views, little appreciation that their concerns might turn out to be constructive in the long run.

In this respect there are echoes of Noble's dark vision of technology as driven by motives far from those of organizational effectiveness. In studying the history of machine tools, Noble (1995) found,

> . . . that while technical and economic considerations were always important, they were rarely the decisive factors when it came to what was ultimately designed and deployed. Behind the technical and economic rhetoric of justification I consistently found other impulses: 1) a management obsession with control; 2) a military emphasis upon command and performance; and 3) enthusiasm and compulsions that blindly fostered the drive for automaticity. (Noble, 1995, p. 76)

Over time, it seems likely that the pattern of use of technology in schools will be set as much by people who have not yet embraced computers as by people who are now enthusiastic proponents. If for no other reason than this, there is a need to understand teachers' use of computers in terms of the daily requirements of teaching. How teachers use computers needs to be understood against the

> . . . backdrop of everyday routines. Classroom routines are not what computers will replace, they are where computers must fit if they are to be useful to teachers. . . . The uncertain routines of computer-based learning threaten the influence of the teacher thus making the transition to new forms of learning problematical. (Olson, 1988, p. 89)

Our colleagues see the gap between their aspirations and current practice.

> We have a long way to go. We haven't developed a strategy on how we are going to use technology effectively in teaching and what the teachers' role is going to be in relation to technology. (Suburban district school board member)

They also, however, report successes.

> Yes, with work and with effort it is there. We have just introduced this software to Kindergarten and Grade 1 teachers right at the bottom end. These three teachers are older (50s plus) and there was quite a

reluctance when we took these machines out. After two training sessions the principal said that he still thought the computers were only collecting dust. So the next time we simply met and chatted about what they were doing with them and what they were hoping to do with them. We spent yet another meeting going through the software catalogues picking out software. We now have that software and it is installed in the machines. They are as excited as hell and this was introduced with them only last September. (Rural district administrator)

It is hard to predict what the outcomes will be. How computers can be used well by teachers is a pressing concern, and this will go beyond simply retraining teachers. It seems likely that integrating computers into teaching and learning will require many teachers to change. The task is not simply one of putting computers in every classroom and then providing in-service education to teachers, although these are certainly important. Rather, the really crucial task seems to be the development and communication of a view of classroom life in which the potential of technology and the most important aspects of teaching complement rather than compete with each other. Cohen (1987) may well be right: '. . . our struggles over such things as . . . the new technology are small episodes in a great collision between inherited and revolutionary ideas about the nature of knowledge, learning, and teaching' (p. 168).

Widening Possibilities

Our colleagues explained the development of technology as moving through stages, and seemed to think of some of the underlying developmental tensions in similar ways. Is the response to technology to be broad and deep, or narrow and at the surface? Their questions echoed De Bresson (1987), who suggested that levels of change can be gauged in terms of several dilemmas. Does the technology involve only the addition of new activities, or are some old functions replaced? How is technology to be used — to change functions, to motivate people, to guide them, or control their behaviour? Will computers change some steps in teaching and learning or the whole process? Are computers to become ancillary supports to teachers or develop into a core technology of teaching? Does technology imply changes in school and classroom organization also?

Seen in this way, the stages appear to involve clarifying a widening range of possibilities, becoming increasingly aware that computer technology can not only change how we do things, but also give us different things we can do (Nickerson and Zodhiates, 1988). The perception that technology enables us to do different things in schools separates some school systems from others. In the survey, 61 percent of the respondents believed that technology would change some aspects of schools significantly but that the basic nature of schooling would remain much as it now is. Two of the four systems we studied seem to be on the verge of a more imaginative and wide-ranging approach to the potential of computers in schools. In one, questions about the role of teachers and place of computers in teaching and learning have recently become the subject of formal policy analysis. In the other, applications have become so extensive in some of the schools that they may have crossed a developmental divide. What seems to separate these systems from the other two may be their willingness to entertain such broader questions, which in turn may be linked to the priorities of their leadership. However these developments are fragile, resting on the views and energy of a few key people rather than being embedded in ongoing institutional processes.

Emergent Goals

The use of technology was most often explained in terms of preparing students for tomorrow's world of work. Over 90 percent of our survey respondents felt it was essential that students understand technology if they are to be employable.

Although it is clear that the world of tomorrow will be more technology intensive than today, this is not nearly so evident in the case of work. Contrary to widespread professional and popular belief, most analysts argue that the impact of technology is neither certain nor predetermined. As we note in the chapter on labor force change, it is not evident that the overall skill requirements of what is called the 'new economy' will rise (Bailey, 1991). For instance, Rumberger (1987) claimed that '[m]ore comprehensive reviews of available case studies find that, on average, skill requirements of jobs have not changed' (p. 83). There is also a tendency to overstate the impact of technology; for example, only 6 percent of US workforce was employed in 'high tech' industries in 1980, and these same industries contributed only 8 percent of new jobs in the 1980s (Rumberger, 1987, p. 90). The same general conclusion appears to hold true in the British and Canadian labor force as well (Levin, 1995b; Roberts, 1995).

Preparation for work aside, the educational goals technology is to serve might best be characterized as 'emergent'. It may be a happy coincidence that, just at the time when some schools are beginning to take seriously such matters as reflective, activity-based learning, connecting in-school and out-of-school learning, and an emphasis on student self-management, we will have the technology to expedite this. As Resnick and Johnson (1988) argue, computers might even help us to change the whole idea of what education is, by serving as 'intelligence extenders', 'conversational partners', information access and storage devices, and problem solving and planning tools, as some of our colleagues suggested.

While it would be regrettable if computers were seen as the only way to change how we organize schooling, these still seem to be developments that many of our colleagues and some of our survey respondents would welcome.

But computers alone are far from enough to foster innovation in the aims and core processes of schools. Innovation involves critical moments when varied factors fit together to create new practices. According to Cohen (1988), to this point technology has had impact only at the margins or where it enhances existing practices. In Nickerson's view (1988), 'If there is a single conclusion to be derived . . . it is that the future is rife with possibilities for major technology-enabled improvements in institutionalized education, but that many of these possibilities probably will not be realized unless adequate attention is paid to the non technical factors that tend to control change in the educational world' (p. 315).

Computers and the Transformation of Teaching and Learning

In the literature on technological change in education it has become common-place to argue, as Mjokowski (1990) has, that the potential of computers 're-mains largely unrealized', that 'actual use is neither extensive nor appropriate', that technology is not well matched to curriculum and instruction, that 'the majority of technology applications in elementary and secondary schools are automating and perpetuating learning outcomes and teaching–learning prac-tices that are themselves in desperate need of reform', and that the need is for 'simultaneous transformation and integration' (pp. 13–17). Similarly, Warger (1990) suggests that there is little evidence about effectiveness of technology (p. vii). White (1990) claims that, compared with other work settings, 'educa-tion has not changed a single basic process that is essential to its operation' as a result of technology (p. 9).

We suspect that our colleagues would find such claims too unsym-pathetic, too impatient, too harsh in their simplicity. They are more attuned to social, political and organizational variables that determine the rate of change. Moreover, many of our colleagues would agree with Rubin and Bruce (1990) that '[n]ew technologies in education are more than simply new tools. They typically require both teachers and students to conceptualize teaching and learning in new ways that must be integrated with well-established classroom routines' (p. 256). Given their training, experience and traditional expectations of their roles, many teachers will find this integration very difficult.

Our colleagues in the four systems seem more inclined to patience, rec-ognizing that although the potential of computer technology may be dramatic, its application is likely to be quite conventional at the outset. 'Originally, the technology is adopted in order to facilitate existing functions and activities. In time, however, the new technology is seen to permit the organization to do things it was not able to do before, and this may motivate a redirection of the organization's business or a redefinition of its role.' (Nickerson, 1992, p. 301)

Technology can transform the work of people, but often doesn't. One reason for this is that it is often used first to do old tasks; it takes time to discover new possibilities. Secondly, there are significant barriers to inquiry oriented instruction in schools — traditional models of teaching and learning are deeply embedded in the structure and culture of schools as well as in the minds of parents and policy makers in education (Cohen, 1987). Old ideas about practice die hard. For example, in contrast to North American reform initiatives, recent education policy in Britain has given much less emphasis to technology than to vehicles such as examinations and inspection systems as means of improving education.

Moreover, the use of computer technology is mediated by traditional relations between manager and the managed (Zuboff, 1988); it is not clear whether information technology will be used to reinforce existing hierarchical and social relationships in schools and classrooms, or as a basis for reinventing these. Computer technology opens up possibilities for rethinking how students learn in schools, not just changing how they are taught. Computer studies is one of the very few areas in which teachers accept that some students will know more than they do. The changes in power relations, in roles and skills needed to be successful in a new environment could be dramatic, but whether these opportunities will be seized is as yet an open question. Among our survey respondents, 100 percent said that information technology can give teachers and students better access to information, and 98 percent said it can expand the range of programs available to learners; both of these uses are consistent with existing student–teacher relationships in classrooms. But when it came to seeing student–teacher relationships in different ways, only 54 percent believe it could give students and teachers better ways to communicate with each other and 75 percent said it allows students to have more control over what, how and when they learn.

There are different visions of what schools and classrooms might become. While a few of our colleagues spoke about teaching and learning transformed by technology, more spoke of the wired classroom.

> We have seen the introduction of laser disk technology into the class-room. We are seeing computers and the advancement of the development of software for learning, right from computer software to the CD ROM technology which I believe is going to surpass the laser disk technology in the classroom. We are now heading into the electronic highway stage in which students in school and at home will be able to access a great deal of research and information that they require. At one time we may have needed a large library. What we have in the library will be so antiquated that it will be like the *High Roads to Reading Series* is now. (Rural district administrator)

There are, of course, apprehensions. Popular and academic literatures are replete with negative images of a '. . . society of monadic, compartmentalized individuals who would end up losing contact with their fellows' (Balle, 1991, p. 93). The potential negative effects of technology are a concern, and addressing these is a good reason to be patient with teachers who have been slow to make the new technology their own. Most of our colleagues are aware that computers do not have simple impacts in classrooms or the social systems surrounding them. Possibilities and dangers exist simultaneously.

Closing Reflections

Computers are extraordinarily powerful machines with educational potential that we have hardly begun to tap. But changes in school organization and classroom practice are essential to support this potential, and our data indicate that school systems are only beginning to consider these larger questions. It may be that technology is not living up to its promise because it has been seen as an answer, rather than a reason to ask questions about the purposes of schools and the nature of teaching and learning.

Educators and policy-makers can make a difference here. It is possible to change the nature of the discussion. One might begin by ensuring that broad questions of the role and use of technology find an important place on the agendas of staff meetings, parent associations, school governing bodies, local authorities and other groups. But these discussions will not help much if they are largely a pooling of ignorance. We need to gather the best information we can about the uses and limits of technology, not only in other schools but in other settings. The potential exists here for fruitful collaboration between the school and the wider community, which is, after all, a first-rate source of such information. Discussions among parents and teachers about their experiences with, hopes for and fears about technology could help all parties deepen their understanding of a wide range of issues. As long as work on technology remains an adjunct, and largely focused on hardware and software, its various potentials are unlikely to be tapped.

In a situation of change experimentation is key. If we don't know what to do, we must try various possibilities, gather evidence about their impact and value, and learn as we go. The use of technology is one of the areas in which such experimentation is already taking place as teachers and schools make efforts in various directions. But the capacity to learn from all that experience is sadly lacking. Most projects are not written-up or circulated. Much could be done at relatively modest cost to share more widely the range of activities being undertaken; if this were the case we might need less investment in reinventing what someone else has already done. Learning organizations require much denser networks of communication and exchange, across classrooms, schools, districts, and countries. Information technology itself provides a prime vehicle for such learning.

In the area of technology, as in so many others, the key will be whether we can develop the capacities to allow us to learn enough so that we are not overwhelmed.

Chapter 8

The Impact of Child Poverty

Socio-economic status continues to be one of the strongest predictors of educational outcomes, as it has been since it came into prominence as a research issue more than thirty years ago. In this chapter we look at the way that colleagues in our partner districts and educators across the province understood and responded to poverty as an issue. In contrast to the two previous chapters, poverty is an example of an issue where the inward focus of schools leads to a limited response to a very powerful influence on school outcomes.

Poverty and Education: A Brief Review

Almost all educational outcomes, such as initial reading achievement, referrals to special education, discipline and behavior problems, years of education completed and grades achieved are strongly correlated with family income. So too are factors that themselves influence school outcomes, such as low birth weight, childhood diseases, and slower infant development. Finally, other life outcomes such as longevity, health status, criminal activity, propensity to political involvement, and so on have also been linked to childhood socio-economic status. In every case low family income is associated with poorer outcomes, a finding that has remained extraordinarily robust in the research (reviewed in more detail in Levin, 1995a).

Educators were, of course, aware long before the research on the subject that poverty had deleterious impacts on education. Programs to provide free meals and health services to needy students began shortly after the introduction of compulsory education in Britain a century ago because it was clear to those involved that students could not learn if they were ill or hungry (Smith and Noble, 1995). Yet poverty has had a chequered history as an issue of education policy.

In the 1960s, poverty was an important policy issue for education in many countries (Silver and Silver, 1991). The United States launched the War on Poverty. In Britain, the Plowden Report attached great importance to schools' efforts to counteract the many negative effects of poverty. As the political mood shifted to the conservative side over the next decade or so, poverty largely disappeared from the educational agenda. Issues of spending levels, examinations, and governance systems took centre stage. But in the last few years poverty has re-emerged as an important education issue. After years of spending and tax cuts, program reductions, and efforts to shrink the public sector, all three countries have seen a large increase in the number of poor children with, not surprisingly, some very difficult consequences for schools. Bradshaw's comment on Britain is equally true of the US and Canada:

> During the 1980s children have borne the brunt of the changes that have occurred in the economic conditions, demographic structure and social policies of the UK. More children have been living in low income families and the number of children living in poverty has doubled. Inequalities have also become wider. There is no evidence that improvements in the living standards of the better off have trickled down to low income families with children. (Bradshaw, 1990, p. 51)

Poverty used to be felt mostly by the elderly, but because of pensions and other changes it is now heavily concentrated among young families, and especially those headed by female single parents (Canadian Council on Social Development, 1992). Child poverty rates are estimated at about 25 percent in Britain, 20 percent in Canada, and 25 percent in the United States, with far higher rates for some subpopulations (such as Aboriginals in Canada or African-Americans in the US).

Growth in levels of poverty among families and therefore among children can be attributed to several factors. The most important of these is the deterioration in the labor market in all three countries. The largest group of poor people now consists of families with one or both parents working but whose income is simply insufficient. Rising average levels of unemployment, falling real wages, and the significant decreases in secure, middle-income jobs such as those in manufacturing have made it more difficult for many families to support themselves no matter how hard they try. Manufacturing employment — an important source of jobs with reasonable wages and good security — has declined sharply in all three countries, especially so in Britain, where according to one estimate 30 percent of dependent children live in homes without a full-time worker, up from 18 percent in 1979 (Smith and Noble, 1995). Wage disparities have grown, so that minimum wages (where they exist) or low-end wages are less and less adequate to maintain a reasonable standard of living. Inequality in earned income has risen in all three countries, and inequality in total income has risen quite noticeably in Britain and the United States (Economic Council, 1992). In all three countries the top pre-tax income quintile earns ten times or more as much as the bottom quintile (Canadian Council on Social Development, 1992).

Poverty rates have not declined despite the enormous growth in two-income families. Much increased labor force participation by women has not reduced the number of poor families very much, And were there not income assistance and other social programs, poverty levels would be much higher, since earned income inequality is much higher than total income inequality in the United States, Britain and Canada. Social programs such as income supports, which do reduce poverty rates significantly, have been cut in all three countries, throwing additional numbers of people into poverty, even though none of the three countries is, by international standards, a high spender on social services (Economic Council, 1992).

Another significant source of poverty for children is marriage breakdown — separation or divorce (which is itself affected by poverty, so that, for example, increased unemployment is associated with increased marriage breakdown). The economic implications of separation or divorce are serious and very negative for women, whose incomes tend to drop dramatically in these circumstances, while those of men often rise (Gunderson, Muszynski and Keck, 1990). In countries where child maintenance provisions are better, and where there are more supports such as low-cost child care available, poverty rates among single-parents (overwhelmingly female) are much less than the 50 percent to 60 percent that is typical of Canada, the United States and Britain (Canadian Council on Social Development, 1992).

These trends present formidable challenges to schools, especially those serving less affluent areas. Poor economic status is associated with weaker preparation before entering school, less support for students in school, and disruptions such as hunger, family violence, and mobility. Low socio-economic status is more strongly associated with poor educational outcomes than any other variable. Yet educators are quite ambivalent about the meaning of poverty for their work and the conduct of schooling.

Understandings of Poverty

In none of the five districts we studied did poverty *per se* appear as an agenda item for school boards or administrator groups, and there were only a few mentions of related issues such as additional programs in particular schools. Poverty may well be discussed by school boards or administrators without appearing in official records of such meetings, especially if the discussion is general in nature and does not lead to any specific actions or recommendations. It is clear from the interviews that many respondents are highly aware of the importance of poverty as an issue in their school or district. Nonetheless, in reading the official records of these organizations, one would not come to the conclusion that the issue is particularly important for any of the districts.

In our survey of school board chairs and superintendents, poverty was given a lower priority as an educational issue than were information technology or changes in work. Only about a quarter of the respondents described poverty as being an important issue in their district, compared with 65 percent for changes in work and more than 90 percent for information technology. No survey respondents said that dealing with poverty was a major aspect of their work, compared with 9 percent for technology and 20 percent for changes in work. At a recent seminar we conducted for school board members in which participants could choose to discuss poverty, information technology or labor market change as important issues, only 10 percent of those attending chose poverty.

This level of attention seems remarkably low in light of the powerful impact that socio-economic status has on almost all school outcomes. Poverty exists in all five of our districts, and it is a widely publicized fact that the province in which the research was done has one of the highest rates of child poverty in Canada (National Council on Welfare, 1993). Yet among our survey respondents, 65 percent believed that the poverty rate among children in their district was 15 percent or less. True, more than 60 percent believed that child poverty had increased in their district in recent years, but it is likely that these key actors were underestimating the real prevalence of poverty in their areas. One wonders why such a powerful influence on educational outcomes gets relatively short shrift in school districts in comparison to other issues that are, on the face of it, much less significant.

Some clue to this situation emerges when we consider the ways in which our respondents report learning about poverty. There is a link, in our view, between the reliance on informal sources of data and the lack of profile of poverty as an issue. The primary source of information for our colleagues is personal contact with other people. In schools and smaller districts the contact is with students and their families directly. In large districts superintendents and school board members rely more heavily on reports from other staff, who in turn have direct contact with students. This process is largely informal and unorganized. Most teachers and administrators come from middle class backgrounds and have, fortunately, little personal experience with poverty. Nor do teachers and administrators tend to live in poor communities. Among the five districts in our study, only the urban district — and there primarily in one part of the district — had some mechanisms in place to make sure that poverty issues did receive attention on a regular basis. If a principal is oriented to poverty as an issue, she or he will see it. If the person's orientation is less to socio-economic status than to family organization, then that is what the person is likely to see as the problem. We were rarely if ever given any data about poverty levels in schools or districts (even though the urban district, at least, collects and distributes such data regularly).

District perspectives may also be affected by the fact that there are no pressure groups advocating with the school boards the importance of poverty as an issue, as there are on other issues that seem to get more attention, such as transportation or special education or budgeting. Political lobbying on this issue tends to be rare. Governments in Canada, Britain and the United States have in recent years avoided giving attention to poverty as a source of educational problems — probably in part because their other policies are factors in increasing poverty rates. For example, the 1995 report of the Chief Inspector of Schools, Chris Woodhead, discussed problems of educational achievement in Britain without referring to socio-economic status as an issue. The general public mood has been hostile to efforts to help the disadvantaged, with much more focus on cutting public expenditure and taxation. A number of factors, then, combine to make poverty a less visible issue than the evidence on its effects would justify.

District Context and Poverty

The extent to which an issue is seen as important depends on the context of the organization, but not in a simple way. On the one hand, poverty is on the whole more often and more knowledgeably spoken about by respondents in districts where more of it exists. However whether poverty is seen is not simply a matter of the statistics on low-income families. It is also a matter of the mental maps of those doing the looking — as to how they conceptualize their organization and their community. In two districts — the urban and the Aboriginal — poverty is widely recognized as an issue, while in the other three it has much less prominence.

In the urban district, with a large inner-city where poverty is widespread, many, though not all respondents speak knowledgeably about it. A rough estimate would be that children from poor families account for about half the district's enrollment, and that a significant number of schools draw almost their entire enrollment from such families. Poverty is seen as an enormous problem that provides a vexing challenge to the district.

> It's a disastrous affliction . . . We, and society, haven't managed it yet. We have a large amount of transience in this district, although it is down from what it used to be, so there has been some stabilization. But the level of poverty has not improved whatsoever and the economic situation hasn't helped one bit. Poverty is incredibly destructive . . . We don't have any strategies for getting people out of welfare once they are on it. (Urban district school board member)

> It is certainly a big issue for me at the school. It is a difficult issue to address because I don't see a direct solution to it. I think it is one of the major factors that certainly impacts on a student's success in school, because along with it come so many other things . . . (Urban district school administrator)

In the Aboriginal district poverty is not an affliction for a limited number of students in a largely successful system, but a feature of life for many in the community. Everyone is well aware of the problem.

> I think it [high dropout rates] is due to the social situation here, the economic situation. There is really poor housing, there is no employment. That's what I think it is. Also, sometimes somebody will say: 'My child is not going to school today because they have no lunch.' So we try to provide lunch here for them — to help the kids. (Aboriginal district school board member)

> . . . Housing and water are problems. There is still no running water
> in a lot of homes. Sometimes people say: 'My kids are not going to
> school because I have no water.' That is the main problem. We've
> provided an incentive here in the school for attendance, and we've
> started a lunch program. I think these work pretty well. (Aboriginal
> district school board member)

However poverty, though common, is overshadowed in the district by other issues,
especially general concerns about quality of education and self-governance.

In the other three districts, where poverty levels are reported as being
much lower, it is seen either as one issue among many facing the schools, or
as largely anomalous — something that needs to be dealt with by schools as
it arises for specific children. Respondents in these settings tend to have less
individual knowledge about poverty. This is also consistent with our survey
data, since 66 percent of our respondents agreed that poverty was not a major
concern in their area.

> We certainly have a number of schools that have a lot of low-income
> populations and we're very aware of those schools. We also have
> schools that are catering to a lot of immigrants, and typically those
> populations are lower income as well. It seems most of this popula-
> tion is in [one part of the district though some other schools also have
> significant numbers] . . . That puts pressure on the district. We have a
> lot more social problems. (Suburban district school board member)

> In terms of poverty I don't think we have very many poor kids, al-
> though we do have some. It's a difficult thing to measure . . . It's hard
> to know how many of those farm kids are in bad shape, some of them
> are for sure . . . I don't see poverty as affecting a large number of our
> kids but I know it's an important thing for the small number of our
> kids that are in that spot. (Rural district school administrator)

> In terms of poverty, in this school in particular I wouldn't see it being
> a huge problem. In some other schools in the district it does create a
> major problem. I think kids are suffering when they come to school
> without proper food, the parents of many children in the junior high
> . . . aren't home when the kids go home, alcohol creates a problem,
> many are on social assistance, kids can't get involved in extra-curricular
> activities that cost money so schools try to develop programs that won't
> cost money. (Suburban-rural district school administrator)

As noted earlier, these remarks probably understate the real incidence of
poverty in these districts. In the rural/suburban district and even more in the
suburban district there is growing awareness of the issue.

I am also noticing major economic problems for our students. We are noticing an increase in students working to stay in school where in 1967 students had little part-time jobs to help the allowance, it was basically for pocket money. Now students are working because they have to work. The breadwinner's job is in jeopardy and these young people just do not have financial resources. Government sources of money have nearly dried up for kids in high school, so it is becoming more and more of a problem. (Suburban-rural district school administrator)

Up until the last five to eight years, you probably could have identified which schools in the district would have children that would have poverty as an issue in their life. There were schools where that would not have been an issue at all. What we are seeing is that the issue of poverty and all of the concerns that come with it are becoming more prevalent in a number of our schools. A great number of our schools are getting a lot of children who are coming into group homes whose parents have been affected financially by the economy. Probably the majority of our schools have some element of that. (Suburban district school board member)

For the most part, poverty is still seen as a problem of individual students. Low income is seen to mean that students are less well prepared for school, that they may come to school hungry, that there may be no books in their home, that they may not receive adequate parental supervision, that they may not be able to afford extra-curricular activities. Among survey respondents, the most common outcome of poverty was felt to be inability to participate in extra-curricular activities (88 percent), though most respondents also agreed that poverty resulted in lower school achievement (79 percent), more behavioral problems (67 percent), and less parental interest in children's education (55 percent). If students lack these requisites — what is sometimes called 'social capital' (Coleman, 1987) — they are likely to have difficulties at school. Within this frame, our colleagues noted a number of ways in which poverty manifests itself, ranging from relatively simple matters such as inability to pay for extra-curricular activities, to behavioral problems, to secondary school students being forced to support themselves.

Sometimes I marvel at the success of the students. What our schools are attempting to do is to make it easy for them to identify themselves as being in need in a discreet manner, then we provide them with support. We do that in a variety of ways. If there are students who could succeed with a small amount of income, we try to help them find a part-time job. If there are students who are already working and simply don't have the wherewithal to pay all the expenses, we will attempt to find some assistance for them, maybe through a bursary fund. If some students come to the school hungry, they do know where to go for some food, which again is provided in a discreet manner through the school cafeteria or some other method. We also attempt to get the social services involved in supporting the students where we are aware of difficulties. We find that more and more students are identifying themselves to us knowing that their cases are handled confidentially. So, I think it has been quite successful. (Urban district administrator)

When I was looking at the program for this year it really struck me that people must really be suffering out there. For some reason we seem to have had more fights in the school. I have no idea if that has to do with economics. In other schools there are more families in crisis and needing help . . . (Suburban-rural district school administrator)

Many of our colleagues speak of poverty primarily as an issue of family breakdown, which we explore more fully in Chapter 9.

I don't believe that the poverty we have around here is financial. Whenever we ask for contribution for a field trip, for example, when we are going to a concert, we have very little difficulty in getting the money because parents endeavor to pay to enable their children to have the experience. So in that kind of context I don't believe that the poverty is essentially around money. But there is a poverty of life — the lack of enrichment in the family, lack of hope, the hopelessness that is caused through generations of not working, generations sustaining themselves on the public purse and never knowing what it is to have a person from the family who goes out to work, and come home with benefits of doing that work. That is the kind of poverty I am talking about — the poverty of not having books, the poverty that is caused through the breakdown of the family, violence of frustration and hopelessness. (Urban district school administrator)

Survey respondents saw a variety of factors as causing poverty. The single item receiving the highest level of support was welfare dependency (79 percent), and 60 percent also rated births to young single mothers as a cause, both consistent with views currently promoted by many governments that the poor are responsible for their own fate. However other causes seen as important by most respondents to our survey of school board chairs and superintendents were low wage levels (77 percent), lack of employment opportunities (75 percent), marriage breakup (57 percent) and racism (57 percent). An especially interesting finding arises in regard to single parent families. A significant number of our colleagues mentioned single parent families as a source of problems for students. The evidence shows that in Canada about 60 percent of female-headed single parent families are living on incomes below the poverty line (National Council of Welfare, 1993). In the US the rate is even higher, while in Britain it is less than half as much (Canadian Council on Social Development, 1992). Yet only two respondents noted that in their view family structure was less important than income or other variables. The picture that respondents develop is thus largely affected by their preconceptions.

Responses to Poverty

Given the diversity in ideas about the extent and causes of poverty, it is not surprising that we found uncertainty and mixed opinion about the degree to which school districts ought to be responding to the issue. Some feel that the social mandate of schools is inappropriate. Fifty percent of our survey respondents either agreed or were neutral on the suggestion that 'schools should not be responsible for dealing with problems of poverty'.

> Schools already do too much. I think people in the community feel that way too. Teachers are expected to do too much, we shouldn't have to feed, we shouldn't have to clothe, kids shouldn't be sentenced to school by the justice system, we shouldn't have to do all the social aspects, but then they'll say, somebody has to do it. There's a feeling that if only those governments could figure this out so that teachers could concentrate on teaching, things would be better. (Urban district school board member)

> I would also say that poverty is seen not as a school problem, that is, not a problem that can be solved by the school. (Suburban district administrator)

> I do not think the schools can do any more than they are doing. We often put the basic education on the back burner for a while and a lot of this stuff that we are trying to do preventive work for creeps in. Even though I am working in that area, I do not think it is right that we have to spend so much time in the school trying to solve all the problems that have happened outside of the school. That is exactly what we are faced with. (Rural district school board member)

But others see no way for schools to avoid the issue, even if they are troubled by it.

> I see the school as the only institution in the society that has a captive audience for 5½ hours a day. So, as well as educating the kids, we are also given the mandate to feed, clothe, house and counsel them etc. I have no problem with having to do these, what I resent is that the resources that enable us to do them are being taken away, and the

fundamental causes of these things are never addressed. (Urban district school administrator)

Most of our colleagues believe that the regular academic work of the school cannot be done unless basic social needs are met.

Research studies identify primary needs and demonstrate that it is difficult to focus on secondary needs until you satisfy the primary need. Consequently it is very difficult for students here to focus on education needs when in fact they do not know where they will be living the next day, and when they will be eating. (Urban district school administrator)

And some colleagues noted that the schools had themselves assumed the mantle of an anti-poverty agency.

. . . for a long time schools were able and willing to take on more and more. Many teachers have a strong social conscience and they identified needs in a child and were determined to meet those needs. Other agencies have built on this pattern and said let's try to push a service on to the school system. On the other hand we've probably voluntarily taken on things like this. For example, we knew the kids were coming to school very hungry and so they weren't being productive in school, so we took on a Nutrition Program. Maybe it was easier for us just to implement a program than it was for us to fight with somebody else to get them to take it on. (Urban district administrator)

All the districts have taken some steps to address issues of poverty. Their efforts are defined largely within a frame that sees poverty as a problem of individual students and their ability to meet the demands of schools. In two of the districts the response to poverty is at least partly coordinated at the district level, while in the other three the problem is seen largely as a responsibility of individual schools with the district assisting in various ways. None of the districts has what could be called a plan or strategy on the issue, though the urban district does have a range of programs. The individualistic orientation to poverty as an issue means that most efforts focus around providing extra resources to schools so that they can in turn provide programs for children that will compensate for the limitations of their home lives. Although 85 percent of our survey respondents agreed that schools with significant numbers of poor children require additional resources, much of the school response to poverty depends on the orientation, energy and commitment of principals and teachers.

No, it's not taking a leadership role or an initiative situation. It's hoping that the parents would come forward with something like that we could support. It was at the initiative of the parents committee at [one school] that a lot of these developments went forward. It was also at a time when we had a lot more financial resources. It may be difficult to start a lot of those initiatives in the current economic climate. (Suburban district school board member)

Again I think that because it is largely unstated the principals are given a fair amount of latitude to try to work out what they feel is the best in their own community. Then they come to the superintendent's department and request additional supports where they feel that they can legitimately get them, like in resource or support staff, possibly in lunch or breakfast programs. I guess the rest they do within their own community. (Suburban district administrator)

The most common — practically universal — responses are school budgets and policies to ensure that children can participate in school activities regardless of family ability to pay. All the districts make at least some provision for schools to pay for various activities such as field trips or musical instruments for students who would otherwise not be able to afford them.

[W]e have been aware of the importance of recognizing the difficult financial circumstances of a lot of families. For instance, we have been re-examining our field trip policies and trying to make sure that school trips are affordable to all people . . . That's the kind of thing we see. In terms of holding back on user fees, we haven't changed any of our policies in that area, but we've been very concerned about extra curricular types of trips or activities which might be difficult for low income families. (Suburban district school board member)

The churches provide the school with funds for any activity for a child whose parents cannot afford field trips, for example. So no child misses out on any activity because of not having the dollars to take part. (Rural district administrator)

Most districts also mention guidance and counselling services as a response to students with difficulties, whether caused by poverty or not.

. . . The board supports a breakfast program at [one] school, and has also provided extra staff, a full time guidance counsellor and a resource teacher, so there has been some input where it is needed. In [this community] poverty is not that visible. At [another school] where I was previously, we had a full time resource teacher, a full time guidance counsellor, and we also had a community liaison worker, and, through a grant from the government we had a staff person who would work with students who needed extra help. Many of those students came from low income backgrounds and many were experiencing social problems in the home. The staff person would visit the homes in August and ensure that the students had the supplies and clothing necessary to start school in September. (Suburban-rural school administrator)

Some districts were attempting to work collaboratively with other social service and community agencies, an issue discussed more fully in the next chapter.

We are trying to implement a student assistance program . . . What we want is for the various agencies in town . . . to work together and to approach these individuals as a unit. As a school we have gotten these people together twice now because it is a community concern. (Rural district school administrator)

Although these are the most common measures, districts were trying other approaches. Four of the districts are providing, at least in some schools, services such as meal programs or winter clothing to needy students. The suburban district has one school which has made an important effort in working more closely with parents and families.

In my mind [one school] has been a shining example of overcoming some of those problems. The active involvement of the parents and the school has resulted initiatives that help the school to develop programs to fight racism, to give support to single parents in terms of day care and before and after school programs, to assist in the early identification programs for students to regain some advantages in education, to provide community liaison workers to work with immigrant parents to learn more English and to increase employment opportunities. Those are the kinds of things a lot of us would like to see more of. (Suburban district school board member)

Still, the predominant response in these districts is low key and local, and coupled with some uncertainty as to whether schools can be effective in this area.

We try, to a limited extent, to give help to students. (Suburban district school board member)

The exceptions to this pattern occur in the urban district and the Aboriginal district, and it is worth looking at each of these in more detail.

The Urban District

In the urban district, widespread agreement on the importance of poverty is not necessarily matched by a clear sense of strategy as to how to deal with the problem.

I'm not sure we know how [to address poverty]. We do talk about it a lot, but we don't have a grasp of how to deal with it. (Urban district administrator)

I think this Board is genuinely trying to hold with programs that try to address poverty. I think there is a pride that this district has a history of trying to deal with poverty in a substantive way. Even here though we're not doing a very good job. (Urban district school board member)

However the district has recognized the existence of educational problems in the inner-city for more than twenty years, and has developed a set of programs and practices around those conditions. For example, it provides extra resources to schools characterized as inner-city, and does have an array of programs and services related to poverty. These include lunch and breakfast programs, summer enrichment programs, the only nursery program (for 4-year-olds) in the province to be supported by a school district, housing registries in some schools to try to reduce student mobility, special 'migrancy programs' for students who change school frequently, and others. Many school and district communications are translated into the variety of languages spoken by students and parents. The district has also supported an organization that hires local people as community workers to help connect inner-city schools with parents. The district budget figures show that several million dollars — perhaps as much as 5 percent of its total operating budget — are provided in additional support to inner-city schools.

Despite these measures, our colleagues in the district are well aware that problems of poverty are continuing, if not increasing, leading to some tension between what is being done and what might be needed. The district is facing severe budget pressures due to restricted provincial funding. Many of the anti-poverty programs have been raised as possible areas to cut in order to protect what are considered to be more basic school programs. Although to this point the range of programs has largely survived, the future is uncertain. Can the district do more, especially given constant budget cuts? Should it do more? Can it even sustain its current efforts?

We have an Inner City Superintendent and a number of Inner City schools which primarily get their designation from poverty as poverty manifests itself as unemployment data, or welfare data. The schools are ranked in accordance with the data. We have extra funding for those schools. The staff input in this area is about sixty teachers more for an equivalent population, and sixty teachers is $3 million. There are nutrition programs and all sorts of other supports. Is this a bottomless pit? Probably. Is this a pit where you shouldn't be throwing any dollars? No. What's the appropriate amount of dollars to spend? How much change have you got in your pocket? Spend everything you can to try to give those kids a break. I look at those kids and say if I had to grow up in the environment that some of these kids grow up in I never would have made it. I wonder how do these kids even survive. I have a lot of compassion and sympathy for these kids. I think there's some abominable conditions in which these kids live, and I think we need to do all we can to give them at least a fair break and a decent start. I know of no other way to do that other than through extra resources. The Government recognizes that this is an inner city district and does provide some compensatory funding in that area. The resources are a dilemma, there never are enough in any system. You try to strike a balance and I think what we've done is quite reasonable. Out of [our] budget we spend in the area of [4 to 5 percent] on extra support. (Urban district administrator)

Only in the urban district did one or two respondents say that schools need to reconceive their role so that dealing with issues of poverty is integral to what the school does.

Many of the people working in inner city schools see themselves not just as educators but also involved in social change for children and communities. They are not just looking at what goes on in the classroom from an academic point of view, but looking at a broader scenario and putting programs such as conflict resolution into place to deal with issues that perhaps other districts might say are not within the purview of the school . . . I think they see change within the district a bit differently than other districts do. (Urban district administrator)

So we are trying to tackle all of these big issues simultaneously, learning in schools, the social context in which the children live, so that they can benefit from what the school has to offer. It doesn't really tie into poverty specifically, but asks who are the children, and what do they bring school and how can we respond to what they bring. (Urban district school administrator)

However at the time our study concluded the district had not taken additional systemic steps to focus on the issue of poverty.

Aboriginal District

Unlike other districts, there is no debate among the Board of the Aboriginal district as to whether dealing with poverty is an issue within their mandate. The school community is not separated from the general community, so the problems of the latter are always seen as issues for the former. The district has implemented a number of programs, chiefly around provision of food and clothing, to try to remedy some of the effects of poverty in the community.

We are very much aware that there is child poverty here. [We] have initiated a nutritious snack program because some of the students come to school without breakfast. At Christmas time last year, instead of giving the kids from Nursery to Grade 6 toys and little trinkets, we gave them scarves, tunics, and gloves to help them keep warm in school especially when they play outside. We did this because we noticed that a lot of the kids have nothing to cover their heads, and their fingers are cold in the winter. We also extended our incentive program, now all students from Grades 7 to 12 are included in the program . . . If you attended twenty days of school you got 40 dollars, if you missed one day, it was less 5 dollars unless you had a good reason like you were sick. We did this because I found out we were losing kids in Grade 7 with regard to attendance and dropout . . . We introduced the program to help families that have little or no income. (Aboriginal district school board member)

In this community the school board is and sees itself as a major economic factor through its employment of residents, its sponsorship of students into post-secondary programs, and its purchase of services. In addition to sponsoring people into a teacher-training program in the community, the school also hires local people as teacher aides, bus drivers, maintenance workers, and secretaries. All of these activities are regarded by the school board members not simply as things to be done as efficiently as possible, but as ways in which the school contributes to the overall welfare of the community. In no other district did we find this same sense of the school system itself as a generator of economic activity for the local community.

At the same time, poverty did not come through in our discussions as a major theme in the work of the Aboriginal district. Perhaps because poverty is so widespread in this community, it is taken for granted. We found more focus on creating a system of education for all their students that is of equal quality to that of the white society. Particularly important in doing so is the movement of authority, including control over education, from the federal government to the Band.

Taken as a whole, the set of policy and program responses in the Aboriginal district is still largely organized around a deficit model in which the school will provide extra services for poor children but the major elements of schooling do not change.

Barriers to Action

Our survey data revealed that many colleagues see the current set of responses to poverty as generally adequate. In the areas of information technology and labor market change, as shown in earlier chapters, we found large gaps between strategies that survey respondents thought would be effective, and the

Table 8.1: Strategies for dealing with poverty

	Effective	Implemented
Provide specialized programs for students having difficulty	100	96
Work more closely with parents and the community	100	77
Strengthen ties with other social service agencies	96	73
Strengthen academic programs for all children	91	78
Add supplementary programs such as providing meals or clothing	91	41
Strengthen pre-school education programs	91	28
Extra resources to schools with high concentrations of poor children	83	56
Have more testing of students to identify problems	52	59

Note: Percent of survey respondents

strategies they were actually using in their schools. In a number of instances more than 50 percent of respondents rated practices as effective and also said they were not using them. In other words, there was a sharp sense that more could and should be done. In the case of poverty this gap was much smaller, as shown in Table 8.1.

Unlike the issues of technology and labor force change, most of those reporting a strategy as effective in coping with poverty also identified it as in place in their district. The only significant gap was in the area of supplementary programs such as meals or clothing. The data also reveal the anomalous situation of a strategy — testing — that is implemented more widely than it is thought to be useful! We conclude that districts largely see their current efforts in this area as adequate, related to what is, in our view, the underemphasis in many settings on the importance of poverty as an issue.

In contrast, a growing literature on poverty and education points to a wider set of strategies that schools could use. Three of these are mentioned most frequently. The first is to ensure that disadvantaged students receive as challenging a level of instruction as other students (Knapp, Turnbull and Shields, 1990). Often this means moving away from pull-out programs and curriculum with lower expectations (such as non-academic tracks in secondary schools), both of which are frequently found in schools with large numbers of poor children (Haberman, 1991). A whole series of programs has empirical support in terms of effectiveness in high poverty schools (Herman and Stringfield, 1995). We heard very little discussion of any of these options in the districts we studied. Inner-city educators in the urban district are starting to think about different approaches to instruction, but had not, to our knowledge, tied into the research base.

A second strategy is expanded provision for early childhood education (Karweit, 1989; Barnett and Escobar, 1987; Stein, Leinhardt and Bickel, 1989;

Slavin *et al.*, 1994). The urban district in our study does offer programs for 4-year-olds, a service originally aimed at inner-city children but now offered across the district. All indications are that budget pressures will cause cuts in preschool education provision rather than any expansion or enrichment. None of the other districts was working or appeared to have any intentions of working in this area.

The third policy approach in dealing with poverty is a much stronger connection with parents, families and communities (Nettles, 1991). This strategy assumes that the school cannot stand apart from the community, and must work closely with parents and others to ensure not only that schools are good places for young people, but that the school contributes to the overall economic and social welfare of the community. In our study some elements of this view were present in the urban district and the Aboriginal district. One school in the suburban district was also working with this approach in mind. But in none of the districts is this approach a fundamental aspect of policy. A considerable number of educators, too, see parents and families as responsible for the problems students may bring to school.

Maynes (1993), in studying the educational response to poverty in Edmonton, Canada, suggests three reasons why school districts have not been more active on the issue. First, educators see poverty as outside the mandate of the schools. As has been noted, many of our colleagues shared this view. Even in districts that are trying to address issues of poverty, many respondents do so only because no other agency seems willing to do so and they cannot avoid its impact on their students. Only a few of our colleagues spoke with a sense of advocacy and commitment about the need for schools to work on issues of poverty, though almost all sympathize with the plight of poor children.

A second factor noted by Maynes is the lack of a sense of strategy as to how to address poverty. The administrators and trustees he interviewed could not identify a set of policies and practices that would constitute the basis for addressing poverty issues in schools. This view, too, surfaced in our interviews, even in the urban district which is devoting substantial resources to the problem. Our colleagues do not see how the schools can tackle issues of family income, unemployment, or poor housing. Among survey respondents, only 30 percent disagreed with the statement that schools were unlikely to be successful in ameliorating the effects of poverty. Mandate is relevant here, too, of course. School districts clearly see their primary responsibility in terms of traditional teaching and learning functions. They believe they know how to do these things, but don't know how to tackle wider social issues. We have already argued that there are steps that schools can take; our inclination is to see the lack of sense of strategy as an outgrowth of the lower priority given to the issue. More commitment could generate more ideas about what to do.

Finally, Maynes cited the lack of organized political pressure on school districts as a reason for less attention to poverty. Our review of school district documents found that boards and administrators did devote time to issues that were placed on their agenda by external groups, and that there were few if any such groups lobbying around poverty. The exception is in the urban district where several advisory councils do raise issues connected with poverty on a regular basis.

We would add to Maynes' list the issue of resources. Discussions of resources play a critical role in determining the fate of every issue facing school districts, especially when budgets are steadily diminishing. One's view of available resources depends, of course, on one's sense of priorities, but the reality of schools is that new initiatives or directions may be particularly difficult given shrinking resources. In the urban and suburban districts budget pressures were cited by several respondents as a key barrier to stronger action on poverty. Sixty-four percent of our survey respondents felt that they lacked the resources to do more about poverty.

Conclusion

We see poverty as a particularly interesting issue for several reasons. Economic deprivation has profound impacts on educational outcomes (although not all our colleagues fully recognize this relationship). The impacts of poverty are very visible in many schools, and change the whole nature of some schools. Yet the response of school systems to the issue is muted.

We believe that the main reason for the limited emphasis is that poverty is still not really seen as an educational issue. Many of our colleagues often wish it would go away so they could get on with their real work of teaching the curriculum. The general ideological climate is hostile to such work. Especially given financial and other political pressures, the willingness to try to tackle problems related to poverty is limited.

To be sure, the problems are formidable. Schools are not responsible for, and cannot be expected to solve problems of poverty, which are firmly rooted in the more general social and economic structures of our society. At the same time, we believe that more could and should be done around this issue because its effects are so profound (Levin, 1995a). We have found some educators who take this mission very seriously. For example, one principal in the urban district has taken a strong community economic development approach in her school. To take one instance, students run a food co-op, which is tied to their school work in areas such as mathematics, science and health. Their mothers buy food at the co-op, paying less than they would at local 'convenience' stores. The school is starting to provide nutrition and food preparation information to students and parents to improve diets. Stronger relationships are being built with the community, money is being kept in the community, parent skills are being strengthened, students are learning the formal academic skills but also about working for the benefit of their neighborhood. This example is not unique; in all the districts there are educators who take these concerns seriously and act on them. The Australian Disadvantaged Schools

Program (Connell, White and Johnston, 1991) provided a strong approach to meeting issues of poverty in many schools over a number of years. But these efforts are not yet sufficiently recognized and supported by systemic attention to poverty as an issue.

Chapter 9

Changing Families

We were aware when our research began that important changes in families were occurring in many countries, and that these changes have powerful implications for schools. We decided not to include family change as one of the three central issues in the study largely because it was so amorphous and so hard to define in specific terms.

Our colleagues changed our view of this issue. No other external issue received as much or as heartfelt comment in the five school districts as did changes in families. For educators, these changes are central to their sense of how the world is changing, what these changes mean for schools, and how schools might respond. These are the issues to be examined in this chapter. However because we did not define this issue at the outset as a focus, the data are of a different nature than in the three previous chapters. We have no survey data from school board chairs and superintendents, and we were less active in initiating and exploring the issues in our interviews and document analyses. There is also some overlap between this issue and the earlier chapter on poverty, so some of the data collected on the former issue reappear here in a different context.

The Changing Nature of Family Life

Few issues are currently more contentious than the changing nature of family life. Debates over such issues as child care, abortion, women working, divorce, and single-parenthood are highly charged and have assumed a prominent place in recent political discourse.

Views about the desirability of change apart, it is clear that there have been important changes in the nature of family life in many countries over the past thirty years. It is also clear that these changes have many important implications for schools. Without attempting to be exhaustive, we can identify some of the most important changes.

It is in some ways difficult to speak about changes in family life partly because the *idea* of what a family *is* has changed, or perhaps more accurately become more diverse. Some might say that the family is in decline, while others might contend that our concept of family has, appropriately, broadened.

Perhaps the most significant alteration has been changes in perceptions of gender roles. Women are increasingly seeing themselves, and being seen as capable of filling the entire gamut of social roles. The drive for independence and equality on the part of women has changed families, the workplace, politics, and most other aspects of contemporary life, although women remain significantly disadvantaged in most sectors and most countries. Naturally enough, changes in the role of women have also meant changes in the lives of men, which have also involved some controversy (Conway, 1993).

One of the main manifestations of the changing role of women has been the dramatic increase in female participation in the labor force. In countries such as the US, Canada and Britain, about two-thirds of women are now working (Canadian Council on Social Development, 1992, p. 10; OECD, 1995), including a majority of women with pre-school and school-age children, marking a dramatic change over the last forty years. The most common family 'model' in all three countries now is two parents, both working outside the home at least part-time. For some time — at least into the 1970s — the rising rate of female employment was matched by rising real family income, but in the last fifteen or twenty years family incomes have not grown in real terms despite more paid employment by women (Conway, 1993).

As more women have entered the labor force, more children have experienced other forms of child care, whether from relatives, informal arrangements or child care institutions (OECD, 1995). A whole new economic sector has grown up here, and researchers are examining through long-term studies the impact of alternative child care arrangements on children's development (Conway, 1993).

Another important change in family life has been the increasing rate of marriage breakdown and of remarriage. Single-parent families were common in past as well — indeed, Canada had a higher proportion of single parents in Canada in 1931 than in 1991 (Vanier Institute, n.d.) — but the primary causes of single-parenthood have changed from death to marriage breakdown, with an increasing number of never-married mothers as well. The increased rate of divorce has been accompanied by many more remarriages; the idea of marriage remains a very powerful one. As was noted in the previous chapter on poverty, marriage breakdown continues to exact high costs — economic and otherwise — on women and children (Gunderson, Muszynski and Keck, 1990).

Related to these trends has been a decline in the number of children per family. Men and women are marrying later, having their first child even later, and having fewer children altogether. It seems likely that fewer children mean more parental focus on each child and possibly higher expectations for children's achievements. The rapid growth in children's entertainment — books, movies, camps, lessons — is one manifestation of this change. At the same time, birth rates are much higher among some minority populations, such as Aboriginals in Canada or hispanics in the United States, so that overall population make-up is changing. And the number of adolescent women having and keeping babies without a husband or partner is a growing concern, especially in the United States (Barnhorst and Johnson, 1991; Bradshaw, 1990; Wilson, 1987).

The status of children has also altered over time. At one time children were seen primarily as the property of the parents, and very few controls were placed on what parents could do to children. Today children are accorded more significance as persons, legally and morally, than was the case eighty or a hundred years ago. Increasingly, children are seen to have legal rights, even though they are not legally adults. Although limited in some ways by their status as legal minors, children's rights are acknowledged in many ways in the courts. Indeed, during the last century or so, the legal system has responded to changes in social values by acknowledging children's status as persons whose legal interest may be separate from those of the parents or from those of the school. The state, meaning government, has gradually assumed increasing authority to intervene in the affairs of families to protect the rights of children. The enacting of child abuse legislation is only one example of this long-term and important trend (Magsino, 1991; Coleman, 1987).

The same sorts of controls have arisen on family behavior generally. The recent focus on identifying and trying to reduce family violence involves action by the state in areas which not so long ago were seen as strictly private. Again, this is connected with changes in the status of women as well as children and changing ideas about what is acceptable behavior in any setting.

People also have considerably more education today than used to be the case. The proportion of the population with completed secondary education or with post-secondary education has risen steadily (OECD, 1995). Whatever arguments there may be about the quality of education, it is highly likely that more education is connected with changing concepts of rights, less automatic respect for institutions and authorities, and increased assertiveness on the part of many people.

It is well known that populations are ageing in the industrialized countries. Though much is made of the disappearance of the extended family, in fact adults are now much more likely to have parents and other relatives alive than was the case forty or fifty years ago. One difference now is that extended families of several generations rarely live together. Seniors are both healthier and more affluent, so more able to live on their own. As well, family mobility has increased so that extended family are not necessarily nearby. Rather than speaking about the decline of the extended family, it would be more accurate to talk about its changing nature.

It is not only seniors who are likely to live alone, however. A large number of young people live independently of — or at least separately from — their families, including a substantial number of high school students. Many of these young people face serious barriers to continuing education or to earning a decent living.

Since families, whatever their form, remain the most powerful influences on the development of children, changes in family life have important implications for schools. The basic organization of schooling rests on a model in which the year was built around the agricultural calendar and the family was managed by a stay-at-home mother who could be with her children before school, at lunch, and after school. That is no longer the case in most families. Parents are also less likely to accept at face value the judgments and actions of the school, and to be more assertive about their children's education. On another front, the declining proportion of the population with school-age children means that the political base of support for public education has dropped; schools will need to find ways to communicate with the large majority of people who do not have children in school. Thus changes in families confront schools with issues that are organizational, pedagogical, curricular and political.

Perceptions of Changes in Families

Many of our colleagues felt that changes in families and therefore in the children coming into the schools were the most important changes facing schools. The dominant sentiment was that families were no longer as strong as they once were and that the importance of other institutions such as churches had also declined.

> **Question** What are the biggest issues the district would have to cope with in the next few years?
> I think it is family relationships. We have had some cases of kids who love to vandalize. We did a survey . . . and found that as high as 30 percent of families are not living together anymore. So, the kids do not have any sense of family relationships or principles. (Suburban-rural district school board member)

> The family is not the same as it used to be and the influence that parents had on the children doesn't seem to be what it used to be. Perhaps that is because both parents are working outside of the home, and there is less family being conducted in the home. At the same time, the churches are less influential on families than they used to be, and they have little relevance for young people. That's not to say that young people are amoral or without religion. (Urban district administrator)

> We are seeing more violence, more transient students in our schools and more disintegration within the family. We are seeing students that just do not have the family supports such as were in place even ten years ago. We are dealing with a lot of social, societal factors. (Rural district school administrator)

Many of our colleagues have a notion of the ideal family, in educational terms. Such a family reinforces the traditional messages and belief system of the school.

We have a rather unique situation in that we have a large Mennonite population that is very strong on education. They believe in pushing their kids to succeed, do well, and be well rounded in all facets whether it is the arts, academics or sports. They are very strong parents. They have a strong belief in education. I am not a Mennonite so I do not know if this is part of their belief structure, but I can unequivocally state that the Mennonite kids do very, very well compared to the rest of the population almost without exception. The parents are very supportive of teachers, pushing kids to do their very best, home work policies, discipline policies, or anything like that. (Rural district school administrator)

We heard the term 'dysfunctional' a number of times in descriptions of families.

The biggest thing, for me, would be the change in the family situation. I have come across a number of cases of dysfunctional families and different family units that have had repercussions for children. Those have been quite difficult. (Urban district school administrator)

. . . In some cases this [increased violence in the school] may relate back to the family issue. I am certainly not saying that all divorces create violent children, but some of these children come from homes in which there has been separation and in addition to the separation there are other dysfunctional factors. These children definitely have problems that they bring into the classroom and onto the playground. (Urban district school administrator)

However some colleagues challenged the conventional wisdom on this point.

I think that the sexual revolution is over and we now have higher levels of stability in the families. However, sometimes the economic crunch disintegrates these families . . . To add to my remarks about the family, the fact that the family is stabilizing makes the school become more sensitive to a more consistent group. You can't simply blame things on a dysfunctional family, because those family groups are disappearing. (Urban district school board member)

The result of the perceived weakening of the family is that schools are seen to face more and more serious problems. One frequently-cited example involved increasing numbers of children who are violent.

I would say that the incidence is increasing. We're hearing about that from all areas. We are hearing about it from teachers constantly we're hearing about it from parents whose children are in classrooms with behavior challenging children. We're seeing it reflected in the number of incidents that are reported regularly to the board by the superintendent. What is, I think, striking, is that those incidents of violence, of aggression, of behavior that we would consider out of the ordinary or unusual are happening in younger and younger children. (Suburban district school board member)

What we're hearing is a lot more of family violence, and what we're seeing, I think, is the impact on children who are coming from homes where there is a lot of stress and a lot of inappropriate behaviors that the kids are picking up and showing in schools. It's having an impact on classroom teachers and the number of kids who are almost uncontrollable . . . It's not just the inner city . . . You used to expect, perhaps, some difficult behavior as children get older, but we're seeing really disturbed children at a very early age. (Urban district administrator)

In some districts a rise in the number of families providing foster care can lead to problems for the schools.

If there is a problem with poverty in this division it is being imposed by provincial agents who are moving problem children and families into the area because of housing and placement. Social workers find families that will keep problem children in rural communities. They become the biggest transplanted problems in the school system. They are an urban problem transplanted to a rural area by our social workers that are hired to do that. (Rural district administrator)

More young people in high school are living on their own.

We do certainly have many of our students living on their own at the age of 16, 17 or 18. They work part-time, study part-time, and really live in a very difficult situation. (Urban district school administrator)

Yes, students leave their families because they feel that the family's rules are too tough, or, more legitimately, because their family is so crazy that they need to move into another safe environment. A lot more students are coming back to school in a socio-economic position where they are on their own. They are 18 or 19 and would have been living at home, but for whatever reason their parents have said that is time for them to leave the family nest. We see way more of those kinds of cases. (Suburban district school administrator)

In the rural district, alcohol abuse was more often mentioned by respondents as a problem than was poverty.

> . . . we have quite a problem with alcohol abuse. We have 12- and 13-year-old kids who are encouraged to drink by their parents . . . it is a problem. (Rural district administrator)

> Alcohol is a major player with our kids. We have suspended several kids who have come to school drunk. We have kids in grade 7 who are alcoholics . . . parents have lost control. A lot of these parents are afraid of saying no to their children. (Rural district school administrator)

In all these situations, parents are seen as either less able or less willing to provide support and direction to their children, with negative consequences for children and for the schools.

> The family unit is no longer the father and the mother and the children with the dad and mom working and all coming home at five o'clock to get together and share the day's events. It is not a common factor in our community any longer. I do not have the percentages at my fingertips. I do know that in one of our elementary feeder schools the number of single parent families is 60 percent. I suspect that the number of single parent families in our own school would be between 40 and 50 percent. That has had a major impact on our students. A lot of the students are facing stress, not necessarily because of a single parent family, it is just that the family unit is very different and the roles that they play in it are very different from the roles students their age would have played in 1967. As a result we have a lot of students in our school who are coming in our doors the first thing in the morning very much stressed as a result of having to look after younger siblings, working to keep the family going, sharing crowded conditions with little, if any, study area or opportunity to work on their work, and as a result of abuse through neglect which forces many of our kids to be much older than their years. I am finding that is becoming more and more of a common thread amongst our student population. (Suburban-rural district school administrator)

> In the last couple of years I have also had parents come into my office because they do not know what to do with their own kids . . . The children say that their parents cannot control their lives and the parents are in my office crying . . . Their kids run them and for so long they have given their kids the freedom and it has caught up with them . . . In our society we have eliminated a lot of structure within the family. (Rural district school administrator)

At the same time that many of our colleagues are lamenting the decline of the family, they are also noting the increased pressure parents are exerting on schools, a topic taken up more fully in the next chapter.

Parents now, rather than having large families, have only one or two children and are prepared to invest large amounts of money on those youngsters. They do not tolerate incompetence or inefficiency or poor schooling. They'll complain to someone very quickly if they are dissatisfied. If they are not satisfied at the school level, they will complain to the administration or to the Board. That kind of pressure is on the school system and the people in the system know it. Principals deal with it on an on-going basis. With the Advisory Committee in place in[our district], parents now feel comfortable in approaching the Board. Years ago that was not the case . . .

[Parents are] more interested and more prepared to get involved. They are also a lot more knowledgeable about education. They are volunteering and assisting and learning about education. When you open the doors, you can't keep parents out. (Urban district school board member)

As a result, educators feel themselves under pressure to provide more and different services.

We spend a significant portion of our time dealing with students and their parents on issues that could be more clearly categorized as parenting issues than educational issues. That has to do with the way kids interact with each other, their social and communication skills, integrity and the acceptance of responsibility. We, of necessity, have to focus on those things. I think it is fundamental for us to be involved but somehow I feel that more responsibility has been thrown to the school in those areas. (Suburban district school administrator)

There have been a lot more social programs that the schools are expected to pick up. I am sympathetic to addressing social issues because I believe it is so important . . . Dysfunctional families are not going to bring up better functioning children if there is not the school or somebody in between . . . School is expected to do it more and more. (Rural district school board member)

There seems to be almost a paradoxical public expectation that all kids should be educated and deserve to be in schools and at the same time the school should be an environment that does not tolerate violent behaviors. If parents believe, as they say, that all kids have the right to attend school, they will also have to understand that this right would also extend to kids who may have violent behaviors. We can't have it both ways where all kids have the right to education and we have zero tolerance. (Suburban district administrator)

As suggested in the previous chapter in relation to poverty, these demands are met with some ambivalence. On the one hand, our colleagues feel that they are being asked to take on roles which they cannot effectively discharge, and which distract them from their central academic responsibilities.

> I am required to respond to changes like feeding kids and developing housing registries. I don't think it is my function to do these, certainly I wasn't trained to do them. I am not sure that the public school should be doing half of what it is doing in terms of meeting social needs. I don't believe children should be fed out of education funds. I believe that is a social service function. I believe I am handicapped in doing my educational job by having to use my education funds to feed kids and employ people to develop housing registries. Those are societal functions that I think belong to other organizations. It seems to me that anybody who has got an axe to grind about anything comes to the public school and says, 'this is the instrument by which we can obtain whatever it is we want to obtain'. (Urban district school administrator)

On the other hand, educators have themselves been in the forefront of arguing for this expanded role.

> The public demands are sometimes inconsistent, but some of that is also our responsibility. Who was at the forefront of initiating life skills education? Mainstreaming education? Promoting technology? Feeding hungry children? I look at it this way: there are sufficient numbers of us in education who are so dedicated to the welfare of the child that we are prepared to accept responsibility that goes beyond education. We feel it's our obligation to do the parenting if no one else is doing it. If the child is going to go home where there are no adults present, we feel that it's our responsibility to care for that child during those hours. But no one gives us money to do these things. We are as responsible as the public for adding to our mandate. I believe that these initiatives are probably a measure of how far teachers' professional compassion goes, but there are some consequences to assuming these responsibilities. (Suburban district administrator)

Our colleagues were left with questions that they could not answer about the purpose of schools.

> Maybe it boils down to the big question regarding who are schools for. Are schools for all children? Are schools for children that somebody deems educable? And by educable do we mean middle class kids who are willing to conform to a particular structure that we want to impose on them? This has become a big issue in the province. (Suburban district administrator)

We found it interesting that we heard fewer problems in relation to families in the Aboriginal district, even though it has the highest levels of poverty and unemployment.

Our people right now have a very nice community to live in — we don't worry about safety and things like that. I know that there are problems that come with development like happens in big cities, but being a small community, such problems don't affect us. . . .

In the high school we never have any fights with the boys. I don't think what we face is anywhere near what happens in urban schools. We don't have problems with gangs, we don't have problems with gangs from other schools coming to beat up our kids, and we don't have problems with weapons. (Aboriginal district school administrator)

Our colleagues in the Aboriginal district do report low levels of parent involvement, primarily because most parents were educated in a residential school system in which parents were excluded from their children's education.

Most of us are survivors of residential schools, and our parents or grandparents used to send us to such schools at that time. We boarded there, and the parents never interfered, they never became involved, never had anything to do with the school. I think present day parents are still following that pattern. It is possible that things will change with the next generation, and the parents then will become more involved. (Aboriginal district school board member)

Sources of Knowledge

As with the other issues already discussed, organized attempts to understand and think about family and community change were infrequent in the five districts. These matters were not major topics for discussion at meetings, for professional development, for data-gathering. Here, too, our colleagues' sense of how their communities are changing is rooted in their direct contact with students, or the reports of other professionals on their direct contact with students. Individual incidents take on great salience even if they are quite unusual. The few cases, for example, of quite violent children occupy a great deal of time and energy, and hence have a powerful influence on the way people think about the entire context of schooling.

I think that one of the major items on our agenda these days is the issue of violence and destructive behavior. As recently as yesterday I met with the parents of a 9-year-old whom we have had to suspend indefinitely. This is the second time this year that I am dealing with these very serious problems and in talking to my colleagues the same

thing is happening everywhere. These students are so disruptive that
the word gets through the system and it is demoralizing. It is sapping
energy from some of our most conscientious people. The amount of
time spent on these cases is so disproportionate to our population. I
am very concerned about this. The parents are frequently very angry
and I must spend time simply trying to calm them down. We are really
at a loss at times to know what is triggering some of these things. We
don't know if it is health or drug related or if it goes back to when the
child was in the womb. I see that whole area as much more of a
problem today than ever before. (Suburban district administrator)

As with the issue of poverty, our colleagues tended to express their concerns in terms of individuals rather than larger social processes. We heard very
few comments about overall changes in social and economic structures that
might be leading to the kinds of problems schools were facing, and the comments that were made tended to be rather superficial.

I strongly believe that a number of societal factors have caused an
increase in dysfunctional families. We have one family that recently
lost their home due to excessive gambling. The VLTs have moved into
this area with vengeance. We have an alcoholism problem, and we
have a high unemployment rate in some areas. Our northern stretch
traditionally has high unemployment, and there's a sense of hopelessness there. We have a number of single parents struggling to raise
families as well. We also have a high Aboriginal population in this
district. (Rurual-suburban district administrator)

Strategies and Solutions

Schools' efforts to respond to changes in families chiefly take two forms: extending traditional services to deal with different kinds of problems, and adding
new services to cope directly with identified needs.

In the former category we place initiatives such as extended use of guidance counsellors, special classes for violent students, revised school conduct
codes, adding curriculum content on nutrition, and so on. All school systems
are trying to develop different services to meet the challenges they see themselves facing.

In the latter category are programs (described more fully in the previous
chapter) such as breakfast and lunch programs for students, the distribution of
warm winter clothing, or the creation of housing registries to try to reduce
family mobility. A number of schools and districts had such programs, especially in the inner-city area of the urban district and in the Aboriginal district.
These tended to be seen as add-on programs or special projects. They depended on the initiative and energy of individuals and on special funding

more than on systemic practices and policies. During the time of our study cuts in provincial government funding were forcing difficult choices on districts, and many of these supplementary programs were seen as vulnerable; the core function of the school continues to be seen as teaching the formal curriculum.

A third strategy, also discussed in Chapter 4, involved schools trying to work with other social agencies to assist students and families, but many of our colleagues found these efforts frustrating.

> What we want is for the various agencies in town . . . to work together and to approach these individuals as a unit. As a school we have gotten these people together twice now because it is a community concern. The individual has to be dealt with and we must provide the supports. But unfortunately, every one says 'Confidentiality! We cannot share any information with you. We will listen to what you have to say but we can't share anything with you.' So there are two people who are willing to talk but another eight who say that they cannot reveal anything to anybody else . . . As a result we are working at cross purposes rather than working together for economy of resources and the best interests of the kid and the community. (Rural district school administrator)

Some respondents did suggest that the nature and scale of social change required a more fundamental shift in approach by schools, but this perspective was much less common than the view that saw changes in families as undermining the real work of the school. Although our colleagues are abundantly aware that families are changing, we saw little indication that school systems are rethinking their ideas about what families are or about what schools can expect from children and parents.

We saw in our partner districts a disjuncture between problem and attention. One would expect that an organization seeing itself facing a major set of problems would invest some time and energy in investigating those problems in order to understand their dimensions and to be in a better position to formulate responses. Such does not seem to be the case in regard to our partner districts and the issues of family and community change. Although these issues are seen as important and as problematic, we found little evidence that any of the districts invested commensurate resources in learning about and thinking about these changes, their implications for schools, and the ways in which schools might better respond. Almost all the official work of districts remains within the traditional frame of understanding of schooling, in which academic work around the formal curriculum remains the key task and everything else is subordinated to that work. Even as our colleagues point out how much more difficult and less relevant this task is becoming, most remain committed to it as the centre of their institution's role.

At the same time a growing body of research has moved beyond this disjuncture and called attention to the central role of families and communities in schooling. Working with families is in this view seen as a fundamental part of the school's role, not an add-on or distraction. Schools and families are seen as 'co-producers of learning' (Coleman, Collinge and Tabin, 1995). Epstein (1995) provides a six-fold typology of school and family ties that would, if taken seriously, change dramatically the way that schools thought about their work. The school change models developed by Slavin (Slavin *et al.*, 1994), or Comer (1995) treat families as key parts of education, whatever the social and economic status of those families. In fact, these interventions were specifically designed to work in communities that have the kinds of problems mentioned by our colleagues.

Work with families and communities is also diverse in nature. Strategies involve much more — and more reciprocal — communication between schools and families (e.g., Bastiani, 1995), programs for parent education and training for more effective work with students, and projects that involve students more actively in their children's school work. As examples of the latter, Merttens and colleagues (1996) as well as Epstein (1995) have developed programs to involve parents in students' homework — not as monitors or advisors but as co-participants with steadily increasing communication with teachers one of the positive results. The area is full of promise and one in which teachers can see tangible and positive results of their efforts. However the enterprise rests on willingess to see school–community relationship in rather different terms than they have traditionally been envisaged, and this in turn requires a level of systemic attention and effort that is still far from common.

Chapter 10

Changing Politics and the Politics of Change

The issue of changing politics is different from any of those in the previous four chapters. Three of these — labor force, technology and poverty — were raised in the study at our initiative, as issues we thought had important implications for schools. Changing families, discussed in the previous chapter, was identified by many of our colleagues as a vital issue. Political change was not named by very many of our colleagues as an issue. However as we reflected on our data, we came to the conclusion that changing politics is a thread that runs through much of what we were told even if it was not given that name. Because so many of the other issues we discussed are connected to political ideas and processes, we decided to devote a chapter to looking at these changes and their implications.

That political processes in our society are changing is a truism, but as with other issues there is some debate about the nature of these changes. Many analysts point to a set of features of changing politics that may be seen as negative: more, narrower and more powerful interest groups, growing diversity in the population, the powerful role of the mass media in shaping political perceptions, and declining levels of public trust in institutions. Plank and Boyd (1994) refer to 'the flight from democracy' — the desire to replace democratic politics with some alternative such as the market as a response to the perceived failures of politics.

But a more optimistic view is also possible. One could note the greater role played by parents and children as well as the increased attention to the professional status of educators, the growing attention to issues of human rights (sometimes defined individually and at other times collectively), the effort to take seriously issues of inclusivity and tolerance of difference, and the diminishing acceptance of hierarchy and formal authority. In none of these areas has perfection been reached, of course, but a reasonable case could be made for considerable improvement over the last few decades. The increased politicization of some aspects of education may be at least partly a result of a more educated population, in which case one of the major purposes of schooling — to assist people in playing an active public role — has been successful. Perhaps this is an instance of success not turning out as we had hoped!

Even more broadly, changes in politics are seen as bound up with changes in social and economic structures and, as suggested in Chapter 1, with what is viewed as a fundamental change in the basic nature of our society. Anthony Giddens (1994) describes what he takes to be the central features of a newly emerging politics — repairing damaged solidarities in society, reconciling autonomy and interdependence, and the rise of 'life politics' in which, as feminists have claimed, 'the personal is political'. Giddens speaks of the need for what he calls generative politics, in which political action proceeds through individuals and groups more than through governments. The public sphere is more broadly conceived than just the state. In this setting Giddens advocates a greater emphasis on dialogic democracy, or what he calls the democratizing of democracy, in which formal political processes such as voting are less important than the ongoing work of individuals and groups around particular issues. He advocates political processes that would foster conditions where people can achieve desired outcomes; build active trust; accord autonomy to those affected by policies; and generate resources that enhance autonomy and decentralize power (p. 93).

Other writers have also advanced views of democratic politics that call for more attention to ongoing dialogue and public activity rather than relying so greatly on elections and legislatures. Barber (1984) calls this 'strong democracy'. Stone (1988) refers to the importance of the 'polis' — the assembly of people, broadly conceived, debating and deciding issues. And Mulgan (1994), writing about 'Politics in an Antipolitical Age', argues:

> Because modern democratic politics makes people the creators of their own worlds, it requires them to question and contest, to build according to their own reason and not that of any higher being or any inherited belief . . . Just as every individual creates him or herself, so does every institution have to redefine itself, and justify itself anew. No institutions are in this sense apolitical: all are subject to democratic questioning, to faction and argument . . .
>
> In this sense, politics becomes less part of the definition of the collective, the nation, class or republic, and more part of the armoury of the self-defining, self-creating individual, continually required to make decisions on everything, including what to eat, where to work, and what relationships to maintain . . . (Mulgan, 1994, pp. 19–20)

In this view of democracy, education plays a particularly important role, since it is one of the primary institutions through which skills and processes of dialogue can be developed. Political purposes are closely related to educational purposes and vice versa.

In the last few years education has had a level of political prominence unequalled for some time, perhaps because it embodies so many of the critical elements of our emerging society. As we suggested in Chapter 1, schools are criticized for being too conservative and too progressive, for spending too much and for being starved of resources, for being too concerned with equality and insufficiently concerned with equality. The debates are heated, often polemical. Governments are busy passing new legislation about education — not always wisely, perhaps. Again, however, one can take a positive view of these phenomena, seeing in a vigorous public debate, with all its faults, misconceptions and simplifications, the opportunity to develop a broader and deeper understanding of and support for the work of education, and in new policies, however problematic, an opportunity to learn about what might work in changing conditions. Political debate and action are also educational opportunities.

Our Colleagues' Views

Many of our colleagues were troubled by the impact of changing politics on their work. Political changes — a combination of increased public criticism, diminished support, increased scrutiny and a loss of civility, conflicts in central direction and school autonomy — were regretted. Most believe that students and parents have become less willing to accept professional direction, that the political climate of education has become negative, that political pressures are diversifying and intensifying, that unions and interest groups have become increasingly confrontational, and that these changes are making educator's work more difficult. We heard often that parents are now more assertive and less accepting of the school's expertise and authority.

> The biggest overall change that I have seen is the involvement of parents in all aspects of the education program; the demands parents are now placing on teachers, and not just the acceptance of what teachers state as being the best for their children. In 1968 you were regarded as an expert after four years of university education, and parents let you go your own way, but I think now there are many more demands on first year teachers and on the administration in general. (Rural district administrator)

> Requests come whether they are justified or not. Our requirement to provide busing is a half mile walk or more. We get requests for exceptions all the way from a half mile down to not wanting to cross the street. Parents are more demanding in terms of programming and services. (Suburban-rural district administrator)

> Although parents aren't as actively involved working with the school itself — meeting with principals, and working on parents committees, etc., I think parents expect educators to respond and listen to their concerns more directly. Parents who complain now expect those concerns to be addressed by trustees, school administrators, and teachers. They insist that the school system should be forced to account for the educational actions that they take. (Suburban district school board member)

People believe their tax dollars are paying for education . . . Parents are expecting certain things from the education system. They try to find out why certain directions are taken, and if they are not satisfied they will go somewhere else and find another system. I see a lot of that. (Suburban district school board member)

And students, too, are seen as less accepting of direction than used to be the case.

We get a fair amount of pressure from kids because kids are not prepared to let curriculum, for example, be yesterday's curriculum. They are either raising issues that they want examined, that are impacting them daily in their own community or nationally or just because of the idealism of someone who is between 15 and 21 years of age. They see things that are happening in other parts of the world, they are very altruistic and they want to look at those issues by talking about them. They want to make changes. Kids are really a force to make sure that secondary schools don't stay in the traditional mode. (Suburban district school administrator)

Yes, kids are more outgoing these days than they ever were. I remember that way back kids were shy. They are not shy any longer, neither are their parents. They now speak out more. They know what they want. (Suburban-rural school board member)

Public opinion about schooling, fed by media portrayals and government attacks, is felt to be much less positive, and in some cases seen to be actively unfair.

Regarding external changes I have seen public opinion change significantly over the past twenty-two years. Public opinion has changed from being supportive, if somewhat disinterested, to being in some quarters almost antagonistic. I have seen the government change from seeing public education as a means to attaining societal goals to attacking public education. I see the press as not identifying with public education as a means of development of future generations in our society but rather attacking education constantly as being unable to meet the demands of the moment. I feel pretty disempowered and unsupported by almost everyone except the parents and the community in which I serve. I see them as being very supportive and aware that we are trying to do the very best we can for the success of their children. But everything that I hear, read and see on television tends to contradict that. (Urban district school administrator)

The biggest change is the public belief in, support of and perception of the institution. This is applicable not only to education but also to most facets of our society such as health care. Public support has faltered considerably. In many cases we do not have the parental support of our teaching staff that we did at one time. (Rural district school administrator)

For many of our colleagues, one of the worst outcomes of the criticism is the leverage it gives to governments to restrain or cut school system budgets. Old ways of approaching problems, premised on the availability of extra funds, are no longer available, but new strategies have not been developed.

(T)he change in the availability of funds has forced us to learn to think differently, and it is difficult for us to change our way of thinking with respect to new initiatives. Until we learn to think of innovative approaches within a milieu of restraint, the change . . . limits the system and it limits the way we think about ourselves. (Suburban district administrator)

A number of our colleagues mentioned the increasing importance of what are usually called 'pressure groups'.

Question   How significant has the increasing Aboriginal political presence and organization been?

Latterly, very significant. We have the Urban Aboriginal Advisory Committee and they put pressure on the Board. [A particular group] pushed the Board for an Aboriginal School. We have Aboriginal trustees on the Board. It's quite significant. There are other Native organizations that have also become more active with the District. Aboriginal groups see education as part of their aspirations for autonomy and I think they saw it as an area that they could make inroads early on in their struggle. (Urban district administrator)

Employee groups are also seen as pressure groups, whose interests are often entrenched in collective agreements.

Constituent groups is what I meant, such as our local [teachers' union], our local [support staff union], our bus drivers, and other employee groups. As a Board we may say that you got a 2 percent raise because of the arbitration process, but you have to take days off without pay which offsets that 2 percent raise. In a lot of districts if you force people to take time off without pay, then they will not be willing to participate in extra-curricular events such as coaching athletic events, or supervising lunch programs. They won't do things that are not specified in the collective agreement. Many of these things have been taken for granted as part of the teaching assignment, and now they're saying no, don't take it for granted, and if you're going to play hard ball and force us to take days without pay, then we're going to do the same. It produces an adversarial relationship, and even if you can give them those days back next year, you've created bad feelings that will take a long time to heal. (Rural district administrator)

Question Those are really tough decisions. It seems that they might have a lot of potential to create real stresses within an organization, doesn't it?
Do they ever! We've had a series of meetings with presidents of the three unions, and they say you can't take out the caretaker substitutes, or teacher aides, you can't reduce anything. We ask them, can you show us how to solve the financial problems? I guess you'd expect that from the union presidents, but they are not saying they understand our fiscal situation. I don't think the associations have come to grips with the economic reality. (Urban district administrator)

The result of the intertwining of these forces is that schools are much more open to public review and examination.

The schools are under a microscope as far as the community, including the business community is concerned. There are expectations that the students will graduate with academic excellence, maturity, social skills and exposure to all kinds of things including technology. If this is not happening there are major questions. (Suburban-rural school administrator)

Well I think schools are trying to survive. By survive I mean remain credible and perform a useful function. If schools are seen as being less effective they won't get the public support. People will start putting their kids in private schools. In most cases, private schools are pretty elitist. When I was a principal a student who had been in a private school in grade 9 came to my school to enrol in grade 10. He had a letter from the principal of the private school which said that the kid wasn't cut out to be at that school. Private schools have the ability to screen the undesirable kids out, but we don't have such a screening system or privilege. (Urban district administrator)

With defensiveness comes resentment.

Resentment is a very strong word but I think it comes in when there is a major criticism of the school falling down on the basics — we are not teaching the reading and the writing and the arithmetic. 'Let's get back to the basics! Let's get back to the good old days! What are the schools doing fooling around in areas that they should not be fooling around in?' That is where there is a certain amount of resentment.

I am all for improvement. However, what do you do with the reality of students who need major intervention before we even get down to mathematics? To the best of my knowledge, we, as a profession, never asked to take on these responsibilities. Never once did we ask to be involved in, for an example from the younger grades, the dental plan, the eye plan, immunization, the whole works. More and more was dumped onto the school system. Very little, if anything was ever taken off so the very nature of the school has changed from 1967 . . .

Some of the resentment comes in when we feel that we are being dumped on because we are the steady anchor in society and we are perceived as having the knowledge, expertise and the background to deal with these issues. There is less and less time for the good old things that we used to teach long ago. (Suburban-rural district school administrator)

But we were also impressed with the ability of some of our colleagues to maintain a sense of optimism.

There are positive and negative pressures for change. From some educators and parents we have positive pressures while from other people there are negative pressures. I think what we have to do is to take these negative pressures and make sure we have positive change as a result of them. (Suburban district administrator)

It's easy to be pessimistic and you have to constantly guard against that. I try not to be pessimistic. The trouble I have in my office is that I don't see the 95 percent of the kids who are doing well, I see the 5 percent who are causing trouble. At the end of the day it's easy to say, 'what are these kids doing?' but I have to realize who I'm dealing with. Most of the kids are a good bunch. (Rural district school administrator)

Centralization and Decentralization

School systems are also facing the political impact of contradictory trends towards centralization and decentralization. On one hand, central governments have assumed increasing control over curriculum and imposed additional testing and other accountability requirements on schools. On the other hand, many jurisdictions are taking measures to move authority from intermediate bodies such as school districts to individual schools. The latter movement, however, runs into conflict with twenty or more years of increasing district control, so schools may feel pulled in contrary directions.

Some of our colleagues, for example, report a sense of diminished professional autonomy.

There was far less central direction than there is now. The District was preoccupied with finances, the hiring of staff, etc. In other areas, it was expected that schools would deal not only with problems but also with matters pertaining to curriculum and staff development. The District began to become more centralized in the late 1970s. At that time we felt that there was a change in how the public wanted to be involved. Centralization has been increasing since that time. [This district] has a strong tradition of freedom and autonomy at the school level, and attempts to bring about greater central management have been very difficult. Although I recognize that some matters are best handled at a higher level (district/provincial), I am convinced that growth and commitment to task flourish when self-imposed. (Suburban district school administrator)

I think we've gone from dealing with things in a gentlemanly way towards policies that are developed, input provided and then modified. . . . I think that those of us who were hired as administrators enjoyed the job as administrators because we felt we could make some decisions and we were fairly confident that those decisions would be acceptable and good in terms of the community. That transition took a little bit away from us. It also added to those who wanted direction and did not want to get into trouble for which they would not have a policy to fall back on. They now didn't really have to say, 'This is what I decided.' They could say, 'this is the board policy and if you have a complaint you can go to the board or the superintendent. I am just carrying out the policy'. (Suburban district administrator)

Other colleagues took the view that schools were more autonomous now than previously. Movement toward school based decision making has also been adopted by districts as a response to diversity.

We have increased the level of autonomy of the schools. We have unique and creative programs throughout the various parts of [the district]. If we had a standard education system in [the district] it wouldn't allow for the same expression of diversity. We have a wide range of programming; ESL, Alternative Education, Heritage Languages. Our diversity is not only ethnic, but economic and social as well. It has been the Board policy to provide a wide range of alternatives. (Urban district school board member)

I think the planning towards a school-based decision making process is an attempt to try and get the schools to be different. I've said to schools in my area that I'd like them to look at how they could utilize their supports in whatever way they see fit. The Board policy should be used as a means to enable, and not restrict, and schools should be given a chance to adapt. I wish the Board could go farther but the issues are complex and are linked with jurisdictional issues between education and health, and education and social services. There's a whole range of things that could be looked at. Many schools are doing things individually, or among two or three schools where there is a will, and I think that's great. If school-based decision making could be put in place more than it is now, and if schools can be given more say over what they do with their resources, perhaps they can respond better. (Urban district administrator)

For people working at the district level there are questions about the future and value of their role.

I see the role of a trustee [school board member] as a positive role. I see us as the link between the community and the administrative level or, sometimes, between the school level and the parent. Our system is very intimidating to people who are not familiar with it. Parents and community members feel less intimidated coming to someone who is a trustee and a member of their community. We cannot necessarily solve their problems for them, but help them work their way through the system. There is tremendous amount of information, knowledge and a perspective of the whole system that you gain as a trustee which a person at a school or parent level cannot possibly have. One of the roles I see for myself as a trustee is educating and informing the community and parents from the broad perspective. I am not sure how that would happen if there was not someone like a trustee to do that. I do not have any difficulty in providing more power or input at a school level. I think that is great. The more involvement we can get at that level the better. I still see that there is a role at the trustee level to do the things that I've suggested. (Suburban district school board member)

School Systems Responses to Political Change

School systems have been trying to respond to these changes in political processes. In fact, there has probably been more response to changing political processes than to many of the other issues discussed in earlier chapters, even though political change was not specifically identified by our colleagues as a key pressure. It may be that political pressures are so direct and unavoidable that districts have simply had to respond in some ways, or it may be that the existence of a political level — the elected school board — has hastened the process of adaptation.

Some of the changes being made by districts were structural, while others were more attitudinal. In the former category, we note the development of advisory committees in the urban district, described also in Chapter 5.

At first, the Advisory Committees were difficult, but they have evolved over time and now they are very useful. They discuss their issues on a local basis with trustees and superintendents. They deal with a lot of issues before they come into the Boardroom and the issues take up less time at the Board meetings. It has also helped to inform people better. Certainly the Advisory Committees have generated a lot of work for the administration, but there is no question that they have been beneficial. (Urban district administrator)

The Aboriginal district had also worked to develop consultative and community based decision-making since its take-over of education from the federal government. The entire structure of an elected school board only began at that point.

Other districts have not implemented formal measures, but were taking more steps than previously to consult with the community.

The whole Board has the attitude that in order to have a good school system we need the support of the tax payers and so we've taken the time to talk to people about it, and people have listened to us. When it was suggested that something be cut, and we advised them of the ramifications of making that cut, the tax payers would tell us not to diminish the school programs. (Rural district school board member)

[C]ommunication with our parent groups and our community has always been an issue and a concern within the district, particularly at the board level. We are looking at some strategies to connect more with our parent groups. We need to be more proactive in letting people know what is happening in the school system. I do not get a sense that the majority of parents or community members really know. What they get, they get from the media and that is often not an objective point of view. We need to be more proactive in selling our public school system and selling the good things that are happening. (Suburban district school board member)

. . . the public feel very comfortable coming in if there is a major concern. It is not just to complain or grumble about something or other, they will come in with a major idea and say what do you think about it? Can it work? They will sit down and talk about it. That relationship has been very positive.

. . . the school board has been very supportive on that. They too are very much in the community. They hear what the expectations of the public are. There is a good working relationship there. The [district] is small enough to have personal contact at that level. It is not as if there is a superintendent's office that you see driving by on the third Tuesday of every month with the blue moon. Pick up the phone and it is there. From time to time we run into a snag, that happens as it does in families, but we work it out. We have the freedom to work it out because the confidence seems to be there. (Suburban-rural district school administrator)

Some colleagues felt that the school system needed to take a more aggressive approach to its public image.

Our sense in dealing with the notion that public schools do not do as good as job of academics as do private schools is that it is bullshit. But how do we fight that? The other day I noticed in the newspaper for the first time, [a local school district] had bought a $600–1,000 ad on the weekend to celebrate ten Canada scholars in their school district. Now it seems to me that the public school system is going to be forced to do a better marketing job of letting people know that the kids at [private high schools] are not the only kids that win scholarships. In fact, probably, the kids that come out of a diversified public school system can compete with them hands down in any area. The fact is that we don't have or haven't used marketing to convince those lobby groups that the public school system is doing a good job with kids. (Suburban district school administrator)

The steps taken so far to alter political processes may be limited, but the change in thinking is substantial. Our colleagues recognize that their political world is now much more open than it once was, and that finding new ways in which to adjust to pressures for change will mean developing the capacity to respond openly to critics and criticism. Though this can be difficult, most of our colleagues also see it as potentially positive.

As public schools, one of the good things about outside pressure is that it has forced us to look at what we do and to question whether we are doing it effectively, whether we need to do it better. The greatest impetus to change in the public high schools is the fact that we have to answer those groups that are attacking us all the time. If they were not out there and were not making those comments, high schools would do what many of them do any way, they would just sit back and say, 'We are doing a great job. Everyone thinks we are doing a great job so why should we change what we are doing.' If it was not for them biting at our heels all the time, we would not sit down and say, 'Well, maybe they are right.' (Suburban district school administrator)

I think over the years there have always been some parents and community groups that have been vocal about education. The change I see is that the District and the public at large are legitimizing a voice for all. I think the most recent change that is impacting on education is the question of ownership for public organizations, the sense, in general, of society wanting more say in publicly run institutions, more value for the money that they are putting into them. As money becomes tighter there is a general feeling that all public institutions should be more open to question from the community and media. Even though we've always described ourselves as a publicly run institution, we are now going through a process where the Board has to come to terms with what that really means, whether that means the information they share, or the decision-making process, or whether it's linking Board goals with what occurs in the classroom. (Urban district administrator)

Well, I think there is something called educational snobbery. We think we know something that the rest of the world doesn't know, and we do not want to share that with them because they would not understand it. We do not see it as our responsibility to educate the general public. We need to move more in this direction. We need to engage in dialogue, to interact with the public. (Suburban district administrator)

The openness to greater involvement does not yet seem to extend to students. Although our colleagues talked about students' decreased willingness to accept institutional authority, the districts do not seem at this point to be making changes in the role and place of students in the same way that they are with parents and other adults.

A Political Future

Changes in political practices raise important questions for our colleagues. Questions about 'who education is for' arose in discussions about special education or the apparent off loading on to schools of various services once provided by other social agencies. They worried about the widening gulf between expectations and resources. They resented being required to implement policies developed at the provincial level without reference to their local circumstances or extra financial support. They saw their capacity to respond positively or constructively to social change eroded by prolonged financial restraint as well as intense and sometimes unfair public and media scrutiny.

Some of our colleagues also saw their own roles as problematic. They didn't doubt their own awareness of local political pressures, their adeptness in containing conflicts, or their ability to 'read' individuals and the overall situation. Rather, they wanted to lead, but sensed that leadership now calls for risks they might not be willing to take or skills they might not possess.

These worries were accompanied by a recognition that the politics of education offered some opportunities as well as problems. Districts were taking steps to consult more widely and to try to involve parents and others in more decisions. Some steps had been taken to change decision-making structures and processes.

We see much potential in this more optimistic view of political processes and recognition of the need for debate about the purposes, nature and shape of public education. Changing politics can be an educational opportunity — a chance for everyone to see what new and improved institutional arrangements we might make (Lindblom, 1990).

The essential task posed by social change is to find ways to broaden educational possibilities, not restrict them. In our view, basic political forces such as the growing pluralism of society require redefining authority structures and relationships, not eliminating them. A plural system is marked by variety, alternatives, choices, and multiple sites of power and initiative, and calls for an enabling rather than a controlling approach to leadership. Increasing diversity has been and can be a positive force for educational improvement, not just a problem to be solved (Riffel, Levin and Young, 1996). These possibilities need much more exploration.

Politics at their best are always about increased possibility, not less. This means going beyond financial and administrative issues and including new ways of thinking about teaching and learning, as well as a widened and more plural view of the purposes of schools and who they are for. Although external pressures are important drivers of change no simple or complete correspondence between external changes and internal adjustments should be expected, or wanted. Schools should be responsive to external changes, and at the same time have their own evolving identity. Organizational learning is not just change; it is also harmonizing education and social change, responding to change in educationally appropriate or challenging ways.

Reframing the debate about contemporary education, to us, means giving as much attention to educational questions as administrative issues. The problem with the present agenda is not what it includes, but what it leaves out. The issues that dominate the current political debate — resources, structural arrangements, and standards — occupy a narrow band on the spectrum of concerns. As issues go, they are administrative, difficult and probably important. They are also educationally sterile and gloomy. They remind us of the description of economics as the 'dismal science' (an appellation earned in the early nineteenth century by economists who argued that the problems of poverty were inevitable). We wonder whether politics and administration are becoming the 'dismal arts' of the late twentieth century.

Can we have positive politics without economic prosperity? Pluralistic democracy relies on participative decision making and conflict of ideas. Prosperity undeniably makes both aspects of democracy easier. Restraint seems to require choices, and leads to a more challenging and onerous politics in which the main risk is that politics will become a zero-sum game.

But it seems unlikely that public education will soon recover the favored financial status it enjoyed thirty years ago, even though public discourse about restraint has been deeply influenced by irrational impulses, one-sided formulae, and doubtful assertions (Barlow and Roberston, 1994; Berliner and Biddle, 1995). We can work for change in the financial situation of schools, but until then we will have to learn to combine limited funding with innovation, despite the difficulties.

With respect to the internal operation of schools, much of the emphasis currently is on encouraging staff participation, empowering teachers and creating a professional, collaborative work environment. These developments are important; it is hard to see how we could have successful education without a strong professional culture and high level of commitment by teachers. Yet professionalization alone is probably not enough, and does not sufficiently take into account the deep desire by many people for a more potent place in shaping the institutions that affect their lives. Should not a broad school democracy include parents, community members, and students in structured decision-making processes (Levin, 1994)?

To respond to political change is not only to promote participative decision making but also to engage in intellectual debate. It is important to devise processes through which people develop more control over their lives and acquire the skills and dispositions necessary to be critical and effective participants in society. We do need to shed the habits of 'power over' (power as domination) and develop the skill and attitudes of 'power with' (shared assertiveness and reciprocity), which is required for the practice of democracy. Elster (1983) points out that politics is not just about aggregating preferences, but about transforming them through debate and dialogue. And Tinder (1991) reminds us that '. . . wisdom is not gained by answering questions once and for all but in establishing a thoughtful and continuing relationship to questions . . . Wisdom lies in uncertainty' (p. 232).

All of this will require new political processes — new ways of engaging people in dialogue over important issues; better ways of coping with conflict; vehicles for using difference constructively to understand and solve problems. These vehicles and processes are only gradually taking shape and will require much work to develop. However in our final chapter we offer some suggestions about starting points for schools.

Chapter 11

Coping with Social Change: Themes and Suggestions

> Confronted by this wave of uncertainty, schools can respond, broadly speaking, in either one of two ways: they can imitate a particular version of the past in order to protect against chronic contingency, or they can engage with and anticipate change through innovation and risk-taking. (Halpin, 1996, p. 8)

In this book we have argued that the present is a very unsettled, but also interesting, time for people in schools and school systems. Social changes — in labor markets, technology, the structure of families, poverty, authority patterns and political structures and processes — raise challenging issues about what and who schools are for, the nature of teaching and learning, the structure of school systems, the adequacy and use of resources available to schools, links between school systems and other institutions in society, and the capacity of schools to adapt appropriately to social change.

Our main empirical question has been, 'How do people in school systems understand and respond to social, economic, political and technological changes in society?' Behind that question has been a normative interest in finding ways that school systems might become more outwardly focused, directing more attention toward important external changes and developing more imaginative ways of responding to social change. As a prelude to the suggestions with which we will conclude this book, it will be helpful to summarize the main conclusions we have drawn from our research.

Five Themes

1   Social change is seen as having powerful and often negative effects on schools, the appropriate responses to which are not at all evident.

Our colleagues believe that the work of schools is affected by a wide variety of demographic, economic, technological and social changes. They see many of these changes as making their work more difficult and acknowledge that, despite their efforts, they are not responding as well as they should. It seemed to us that social changes surrounding schools raise fundamental questions about the established purposes and organization of schools, as well as the nature and processes of education, but we did not see many signs that these questions were at the forefront in school systems.

Schools appear to have concentrated their change efforts on internal issues, even though these often make less difference to student outcomes than external developments. There is good reason to believe that changes in various social phenomena such as those discussed in this book have greater effects on the schools' ability to accomplish their goals than do all our efforts to improve curriculum, or train teachers more effectively, or alter instruction.

Many social changes pose real dilemmas for schools — problems that cannot be addressed within current assumptions or by present processes and that therefore call into question both the assumptions underlying problem solving and the processes that guide it. To say that things are difficult and that we are not sure what to do, however, does not mean we should do nothing. The cost of not changing will be the erosion of public legitimacy, resources, professional confidence, and energy. While change also has a price, especially professional uncertainty and political risk, it does seem to be better than inertia.

> 2   School systems are not sufficiently oriented towards learning about the nature and implications of social change. When a learning stance is adopted, it seems more due to fortuitous circumstances than because of a deliberate desire to adopt such a stance.

Our colleagues were perceptive, had a good grasp of their school systems, and were committed to improving education, but the ideas, structures and processes by which they directed their efforts were essentially inward looking and limiting. Although they feel the impact of social change on their work, the school systems do not give very much attention to processes of learning about social change. None of them could in our view be described as organizations in which learning is the dominant response to social change. The foreground of their concern continues to be the traditional work of school — primarily teaching the curriculum. Social change is chiefly seen as a background factor affecting their ability to carry out this primary task. However, given the scale of change and its impact, we believe that this view must be reversed at least to some extent — that the organization and functioning of schools must be re-evaluated in light of social change.

Some districts engaged in some learning about social change some of the time. In these instances (relatively few in number), a learning response to change was highly contingent, and occurred in spite of obstacles to learning that were generally present in the systems. Just as Herzberg arrived at his two-factor theory of workplace motivation after observing that eliminating job dissatisfiers would not at the same time lead to job satisfaction, we concluded that the factors that led to a learning response were not the same as those which contributed to inertia. This means that simply reducing obstacles to learning will not by itself lead to more constructive responses to social change. Additional variables, catalysts if you will, are needed to stimulate a learning response in otherwise unchanging systems.

One such catalyst was perception or meaning — the awareness or belief that the work of the school system was an important, contributing part of a larger whole. We had both negative and positive confirmation of this proposition. On the negative side, the school systems which had the most difficulty adopting a learning stance with respect to change were the systems in which people were the most likely to complain about the absence of 'the big picture', by which they meant an appreciation of where society is moving and how school systems fit. We have already mentioned the uncertainty among many of our colleagues around these questions. On the positive side, the school district which in some ways most saw itself as a learning organization was the Aboriginal district. Despite the very serious problems they faced, people in this district interpreted their work as an integral part of a wider community process of cultural reclamation and community self determination that gave them the optimism and sense of achievement to persevere. Perception, it seems, comes before information and analysis.

The second catalyst we observed was luck. Important learning opportunities occur by chance. In many instances important changes in schools have come about because of a particular set of circumstances — a person with ideas, an identified problem, some extra resources. Perhaps the disposition to take advantage of luck, of working with the openings that social change unpredictably provides, may be a more workable strategy for learning than deliberately setting out to become a learning organization.

3   Strategies for responding to change seemed limited and unimaginative.

Where social change was recognized as raising important issues for schools, the systems tended to use existing practices or strategies rather than thinking through the nature of the challenge and the kinds of responses that might be most appropriate. Schools tend to respond to change with more of what they do now — more courses, more specialized staff, more add-on activities. The systems rely heavily on the efforts of committed individuals. Many new initiatives rest on that extra commitment plus a little extra money, and are vulnerable to personnel changes and budget cuts. Some of our colleagues talked of the need to think about changes that were more fundamental, but we found little evidence that such efforts were in fact being made.

In *Shadow Work* (1981) Ivan Illich argued that schools have become prescriptive systems of production and that prescriptive systems, especially in government and the social services, produce the desired results only when the clients (for example, students or recipients of social assistance) comply with the requirements of the system. The compliance scheme, which is bolstered by legitimating devices of all kinds (for instance, certification requirements, codes of professional practice, and provincially approved curricula) extends beyond clients and includes workers (in this case, teachers and administrators) as well as governments, both local and provincial. Although the historical roots of this way of thinking about education are deep, and the approach was socially beneficial for a period of time, it does seem to be unraveling. Whether the origins of the new view are to be found in growing pluralism of society, in the postmodern spirit or simply in the natural resentment toward authority that is exercised paternalistically, the educational culture of production, prescription and compliance is under assault.

As we noted in Chapter 10, demands for more political openness and participation are usually accompanied by intellectual openings, and so this shift has important consequences for the way we think about education, not just the way we do our politics. Because educators need to explain themselves, not just assert their opinions, they themselves need to put more care into their thinking — they need a more clearly articulated world view, better arguments, more evidence, and, most importantly the disposition to change when they encounter persuasive views that are contrary to their own. And because of growing pluralization of views, it is less likely that a single conception of education could be effective, let alone be imposed on everyone. While unsettling, the situation does suggest greater need, and provide increased scope, for the educational imagination.

The absence of a single view of desirable change can be seen as an advantage, allowing more options and possibilities. The principle of equifinality suggests that many different paths can lead to the same destination. We need not wait to know the right way before we begin a journey. Whether we focus on poverty, culture, or technology, the same issues are likely to arise eventually. Getting going on something is better than prolonged debate over what that first step should be.

> 4   Learning and change in systems are different than learning and change in individual organizations. Learning processes in educational systems are seriously inhibited by the dominance of conventional wisdom about the nature and purposes of schooling.

The literature on organizational learning concentrates on change as a general phenomenon occurring in individual organizations. In schools, the problems seem to be systemic. Schools are based on a set organizational arrangements so widely accepted and deeply entrenched that schools almost everywhere are alike in their internal structures and patterns of activity. The tyranny of these arrangements makes genuine learning and change very difficult. The arrangements are taken for granted, and so their power to restrict educational development is even greater. We felt that in many respects school systems are composed of good people trapped by conventional ideas and prevailing practice, but not recognizing they are trapped and having no process to bring them to that realization and then take them beyond. Even where initiatives are developed, they tend to be one-of-a-kind, having little impact on the larger system and vulnerable to disappearance.

5   Some of the problems are intractable and many of the solutions are beyond the reach of schools alone. Nevertheless it seems reasonable to expect a more outward looking stance and more innovation on the part of schools and school systems. Moving beyond inherited ideas about the nature of learning, teaching and schooling will be a struggle. Still, we need to do better. People can achieve a lot more than they think, in much simpler ways than they believe.

Somehow or other, schools and school systems will have to adjust to the contrary pulls of their internal and external worlds. Apart from ignoring external change or temporizing over responses, the broad strategies seem to be coping, planning and creating. Coping, which we see as the currently dominant strategy, is most often a way of avoiding disaster, or at least minimizing the effects of unwanted external changes on the organization. Planning, which gets lip-service but little real attention, tends to be a technique for rationalization or control. Both these strategies seem, at least to some degree, inconsistent with the need for more imaginative responses to social change.

The process of creation — asking new questions, finding new answers, approaching problems in new ways — really begins with openness to the possibility of change. Some of our colleagues didn't seem to be open, and so our conversations with them often turned to changes they resented or to rationalizations and explanations for their unresponsiveness to external change. We can understand their feelings. External change often leads to self-doubts, and a common human reaction is to brush them away so as to maintain a stable, positive self-image. Rationalization, even blaming, is usually more comfortable than self examination. And we recognize that many of our colleagues are working under considerable pressure with what they perceive to be diminishing support.

Other colleagues seemed more willing to talk about external change on its own terms, without a need for reassurance or certainty. They viewed constraints as rather elastic and were less likely to treat them as reasons for inaction. External change was regarded as an ally rather than an adversary: a reason and direction for internal change, perhaps even an example for it. So, for instance, information technology is seen as a way to change teaching and learning, which is the real objective. Responding to demands for greater public involvement in educational decision making is seen as a way of opening up the educational system. Taking up issues of the connection between schools and work becomes a means of changing the relationship between the school and the broader community.

Educators might think of themselves as engaged in a process of finding a future for schools. Their educational task is to harmonize social change and their evolving educational purposes. Their organizational tasks are less to make decisions about the future shape of systems and more to create and maintain the conditions that allows a future to emerge. And their political task is not just to address an interest group or the public, but to create a public discussion of fundamental educational change.

The Poverty of Current Strategy

What also seems clear to us is that many of the strategies currently being promoted as ways of addressing the problems of education will prove to be quite inadequate. We put these strategies into two main categories. One relies on external (usually government) direction; the other proposes much more control by those working in schools, and especially teachers. Fullan (1991) has termed these respectively 'intensification' and 'professionalization'. In our view neither of these approaches can work by itself, though each may contribute something worthwhile to educational improvement.

We see the problems of education as being fundamentally problems of thinking and hence of learning. They cannot be addressed except through means that lead to changes in thinking and to learning. Thus strategies that rely on external direction to achieve change will not be successful unless they are designed to change people's ideas; to give people the chance to learn.

Consider the case of decentralization of authority to schools — school-based management in North America or local management of schools in Britain. Widely promoted as a means to improve educational outcomes, the evidence suggests that parent councils or school councils rarely work in this way (Leithwood and Menzies, 1996). Instead, we find that in many settings that parents are supportive of current school practices, that few parents are involved in school councils, that involvement may drop off after the first few years, that councils are often dominated by school administrators, and so on (see, for example, Levacic, 1995). When one considers the very limited efforts made to provide training to parents and educators, to give people an opportunity to think about the implications of the new mechanisms — in short, to provide opportunities for learning — the paucity of results is not surprising.

The same point could be made about other widely-mandated government reforms, such as the introduction of so-called 'market' mechanisms, standard curricula, or intensified programs of student assessment. Each of these could be valuable if it provided an opportunity for people involved with education to think anew about what makes sense and why. Typically, however, such measures are implemented in the old top–down fashion, in which it is assumed, despite all the evidence (e.g., McLaughlin, 1987; Cohen, 1992), that directives from governments lead to concomitant changes in behavior and outcomes.

The alternative strategy — giving more authority to professionals who will then take the right steps to reform schools — seems equally dubious in and of itself. Teachers and other professionals certainly deserve to play an important role in formulating education policy and in shaping educational practice. We cannot have effective schools unless educators are involved and committed. However it seems unreasonable to think that teachers, any more than any other occupational group, will always recognize the best interests of students or have those interests at heart when they conlict with teachers' own ideas, needs or interests. Addressing the problems of schooling is not simply a matter of applying technical knowledge, but of mobilizing the knowledge and skills of all parties.

Some Suggestions

In our suggestions we want to capture the need for continuity as well as change, and acknowledge the difficulties inherent in the realignment of organizations, their values and power structures, as well as the very long time real change usually takes. We value the strengths of our partner districts: they were stable, responsive to their immediate constituencies, kept conflict manageable, maintained confidence in schools and were committed to education and children.

We are also conscious of the dangers in our suggestions of a kind of academic rationalism, a view that the world can be understood through analysis and managed without politics. We have noted a number of times in this book, and affirm again, the need to recognize the tensions, contradictions uncertainties and limitations in human action. While we think analysis is important — more important than the role currently assigned to it in education systems — we certainly don't believe that we can think through all the issues we face in some kind of straightforward and unambiguous way. As we said in our Introduction, we do not wish to provide a recipe, or even to imply that there is a recipe.

Nevertheless, we do have reservations about the ways in which our partner school districts characteristically approached social change. They were not sufficiently outward looking. They sometimes accepted constraints too easily and had a highly conditional view of the pursuit of new opportunities, acting if . . . (there is time or new money, there are volunteers, etc.). The ideas that we heard about the nature and meaning of social change did not seem reflected in the actions the organizations were taking. The most common responses to change were piecemeal projects that tended to reinforce the existing system, not to challenge it. In our view this won't be enough; indeed, will be increasingly inadequate as the pressures for change mount. If schools cannot cope more successfully with external change, the legitimacy of public education is put in danger.

> Ultimately, the survival of public services as legitimate meeters of needs for the whole community will depend on feverish innovation to keep up with changing demands, and new structures that allow for risk, enterprise and specialization within the context of universal provision, structures that match tight overall financial control with real autonomy. (Mulgan, 1994, p. 154)

How might school systems become more outwardly focused, direct more attention toward important external changes and develop a wider set of strategies for learning about and responding to social change? We focus our suggestions around six points, all connected with building in school systems the capacity to think about and work on issues of social change. We believe these ideas are practical and feasible even with all the constraints and conflicting pressures facing schools.

Putting Education and Social Change on the Agenda

Understanding and responding to social change in educationally appropriate ways will require a lot of determination, resourcefulness and political skill. Successfully relating the external perspective to an understanding of the internal workings of the system involves treating a number of questions as a set. What's happening in the environment? How are these events and trends related to the system and its ability to achieve its main purposes? How might the system respond? Does the system need to change in order to achieve its purposes? Are there practices in parts of the system which are promising and should be generalized to the whole? Hannah Arendt called this 'to think what we are doing' (1978, p. 4).

It is important to make environmental analysis an agenda item at all levels of the organization. This need not be too demanding. Simply introducing an issue at a school staff meeting, district administrators' meeting or school board meetings, providing some background information, and having fifteen or twenty minutes of discussion may be enough to begin to refocus people's thoughts. Social change issues can also be part of newsletters to parents, school council meetings, and discussion in class with students. In fact, it is especially important that educators share their concerns with the broader community even if we are unsure of how to address the issues. If dialogues about external issues and options for responding to them are regular features of agendas then they become a more important part of people's thinking — a part of our consciousness of issues, as it were. Moreover, providing data in a meeting is more likely to lead to its being read and assimilated than is providing the same information on paper with no discussion.

Putting education and social change on the agenda of school systems means finding other ways to deal with the issues, items and working assumptions which now crowd out social change. There are many reasons why a system might be preoccupied with, say, financial items, to the neglect of education and social change. For example, school board members may see financial matters as their realm, with education being the purview of professionals; they may suspect the financial judgment and political prudence of the superintendent; they may be experiencing a taxpayer revolt of sorts; or they may be deeply divided on educational philosophy, and so avoiding discussing it. Changing the agenda is not just changing priorities, but also reconsidering the personal habits, administrative logic and political assumptions which the current agenda reflects.

Talking to Other People

Putting social change on the agenda will take school systems beyond their usual frameworks. Talking to other people, getting their stories and experiences, will also contribute to this. However, changing who we talk to doesn't mean just finding new professionals with whom to dialogue. Educators need to meet and talk with a wider range of people. One colleague suggested that 'if you want to change what people think, change who they talk to at lunch'. Educators, like other occupations, tend to talk largely with each other. After all, that's who we see every day. But by bringing into staff meetings or other events people with different backgrounds and views we can begin to open up some of the assumptions we hold and to create a wider frame for defining and thinking about issues. Most school communities already contain a wide assortment of people; the trick is to bring some of them into the school to meet and talk with educators. Similarly, school boards might deliberately invite people from other settings to meet with them to exchange perspectives.

We strongly believe that those in our society who are relatively powerless are too seldom heard. For example, if our concern is with poverty we should talk at least as much with people who are poor as we do to other professionals who provide the poor with social and educational services. Need we also observe that students have perhaps the strongest interest in the adaptation of schools to a changing environment, but perhaps the least influence over the course of educational change? Schools could learn much from talking more — and from listening more — to students (Rudduck *et al.*, 1996).

We see talking with other people as being an important initial step in the development of ongoing linkages and relationships. In many of our partner systems, a lot of effort has been put in to developing institution level connections, especially among senior level administrators. This is useful, but strikes us as ultimately having less impact than developing the working relationships among differing systems that make joint action possible. A lot of obstacles need to be overcome if, for example, teachers, social workers, police officers and parents are ultimately to work together.

Linkages within systems probably need as much attention as connections between them. In the systems we studied the connections among schools were generally weak, and the relationships between schools and the district offices sometimes uncertain. Successes in one setting were often unknown to others in the same district, and even more so across districts. Devices such as administrative councils may build bonds (and sometimes rivalries) among administrators, but connections among teachers and other professionals do seem unnecessarily limited.

Diversifying Information Sources

Few of the districts we have worked with collect organized data about such matters as the demographic composition of the district or the economic circumstances of children and families. Where such data are collected, they may have little or no impact on policy. Schools rely for information primarily on personal and informal contact between educators, students and parents. While this contact is vitally important, there are other information sources that would help build a more balanced picture of the changes facing us, just as annual crime statistics show decreases while media reports of particular crimes lead people to think the problem is worsening. Census data are increasingly available for areas as small as an elementary school attendance district, and can provide a wealth of information about community economics and demographics. A variety of government and other bodies also collect survey data on states, provinces or communities that would be useful to schools. Many studies on young people and families are sources of useful information about the changing social context of schooling (such as those cited in earlier chapters around issues of labor force change, technology, or poverty).

Schools and school districts could conduct their own surveys of students, parents, and the community. Many schools do survey students or parents on attitudes to school, but far fewer include questions that would help the school understand parents — their work, the major problems they face, their support networks, their child-care needs, and other factors that have important implications for schools. Such surveys need not be long, sophisticated or expensive. Data from one's own community also has more power to affect people's perceptions than does more general research. If parents across the country are unhappy with some aspect of schools, that may or may not be important to a group of teachers, but if parents in their own community express the same sentiments, that clearly is important.

Political processes also offer schools a way of learning about the community. Educators may see political pressures as problems to be avoided, but they are also a way of learning about what people see as their needs. For example, the urban district has a system of advisory committees. Some are geographic while others deal with particular issues. These committees can and do raise issues for the school board. Administrators in the district once saw these committees as a huge consumer of time and energy, but now increasingly speak of them as a vital source of information about what is happening that the schools need to know about. Instead of a problem, the committees become an important resource for the district.

Broadening the Debate

Many of the people who believe that education needs to change cite an economic rationale for doing so. We do not believe this argument to be wrong, but it is incomplete. There is an argument that one of the important tasks of schools is to prepare students to fill economic roles and that these might include ideas such as productivity, competitiveness, and entrepreneurship. The future welfare of our society is affected by how well schools do this task. Nor do we argue against the view which sees schools as needing to respond to increasing social diversity — in ethnicity, gender, religion and class. We take exception to these only when people claim that these are the only, or the most important things, to which schools should attend. Exclusive arguments such as these usually blame school systems for what they cannot control, assume they have powers they do not, and distract attention away from other priorities and sources of difficulty. We have suggested throughout this book that social change raises many implications for schools, and affects almost every aspect of what we take education to be. The debate about the future of education needs to be as broad as possible.

Difficult as this may be, schools should encourage heresy. By this we mean the deliberate attempt to have divergent points of view on issues expressed and discussed. We hear much these days about the need for a common vision. But a common vision should not mean the absence of other views. In the organizations we have studied there are almost always mavericks who bring different ideas to the table. In healthy organizations these differences are recognized and seen as valuable precisely because it is important for everyone to have the broadest opportunity to think through the issues.

As we noted in Chapter 10, school systems are recognizing this need and beginning to develop processes for such a debate. But the movements in this direction are still halting. We need to experiment with a range of forms that would bring people into the discussion — community forums, surveys, focus groups, written communication, working with existing community organizations, and reaching out to groups that are not traditionally thought of as part of the school community (Cressy, 1994). School systems will need to improve their ability to use conflict productively as part of problem definition and solution. We will have to sharpen our skills in listening empathetically and in describing our own views clearly. A clear implication of this position is that changes in the structure of schooling will be necessary. The kind of open debate and learning we regard as essential will be impossible if hierarchy continues to be the dominant form of organizing; what people know and can do will have to count for more than the position they happen to occupy.

Experimentation

There are countless ways in which school systems might respond positively to social change. We need to broaden, not narrow, how we think of the relationships between education and social change. At least for the present we might be better served not by seeking a new pattern for education, but by engaging in the experimentation from which, if it is still wanted, that new pattern might eventually be drawn.

This means that projects need to be seen differently. Projects, no matter how unusual the combination of circumstance, commitment and talent, demonstrate that it is possible to do something about very challenging social problems and educational issues. They can also provide a glimpse of the future, a benchmark for gauging traditional practices, and a take off point for more fundamental educational responses to social change.

The real problem with projects is the lack of overall strategic significance attached to them. Their piecemeal and idiosyncratic nature gives the impression that they are to be seen as 'only' projects, and not as fundamental experiments in the nature and processes of schooling, conducted on a system's behalf. We will need better and stronger ways for schools and school systems to learn from each other, and especially to borrow what appear to be successful practices. Vehicles for this purpose are currently quite underdeveloped.

Given that we do not fully understand the changes taking place around us or their impact on us, experimentation seems an essential strategy. How can we learn if we don't try things to see how they work? Yet policies of conscious and deliberate experimentation organized to promote learning are rare. Much more frequent is the belief that a solution has been found and that the only need is to make everyone conform to it.

Leadership

An important aspect of organizational learning is creating the conditions which make systemic analysis and reflection more likely. Much of the literature concentrates on leadership. Leadership is important, but the formal leader is not the only source of either external perspective or internal reflection. All leaders are heavily dependent on others, and in this sense their interpersonal skills and political acumen might be used to support a more intellectual approach to how school systems respond to social change.

Nevertheless, modeling by leaders seems crucial. If we want people to seek out friendly criticism, to express differences of opinion respectfully, to listen to others, to question, to participate in active inquiry, model building and exploration, and to engage in dialogue and debate over time, we need to acknowledge that these will not happen if the senior personnel of a school system neither value nor model them. As Macpherson (1996) puts it,

> . . . for leaders to claim they are educative means they must be able to develop and maintain a climate that promotes inquiry, values problem solving, welcomes criticism, and encourages participation and learning about organisation. Openness to criticism and an ability to learn from mistakes becomes the basis for more valuable leadership action and cycles of reflection and decision making. (p. 94)

An optimistic attitude is also important. Many of our colleagues were apprehensive, if not fearful, of change and what it brought: disruption, challenges to the coherence of their inner world, and a disintegration of their conceptions of themselves and their role. When people allow themselves to become pre-occupied with unwanted changes, they lose the connection between themselves and the external world. People who are afraid of change also anticipate more and more threatening upheavals, condemning it in advance and in a curious way, preparing themselves for the worst.

But most important of all may be a combination of political engagement and intellectual probing. We don't see leadership as an activity for detached visionaries. Learning to think and do education differently is a task for those who are action centered and highly engaged, not for those who are intellectual bystanders.

Conclusion

In our account of schools coping with social change we have tried to balance criticism with understanding and support; analysis of problems with optimism about improvement. Some readers may find us too critical, and others too optimistic. We believe that education must be an optimistic endeavor. The whole idea of education rests on the possibility of betterment. One couldn't be an educator if one didn't believe this.

We don't think the challenges are simple ones. The human capacity to comprehend the world, and to act in accord with our comprehension, is in many ways quite limited. In other ways, however, it is remarkable. We choose to focus on the positive potential, the ability of people when motivated and supported to find ways of being in the world that are more conducive to creating and sustaining the kind of schools, and the kind of society, that most of us would want.

References

ARENDT, H. (1978) *Thinking: Volume II, The Life of the Mind*, New York, Harcourt Brace Jovanovich.

ARGYRIS, C. (1992) *On Organizational Learning*, Cambridge, MA, Blackwell.

ASHTON, D. and LOWE, G. (Eds) (1991) *Making Their Way: Education, Training and the Labour Market in Canada and Britain*, Milton Keynes, Open University Press.

ASHTON, D. and MAGUIRE, M. (1987) 'The structure of the youth labour market: Some implications for education policy', in THOMAS, H. and SIMKINS, T. (Eds) *Economics and The Management of Education*, Lewes, Falmer Press, pp. 193–201.

BAILEY, T. (1991) 'Jobs of the future and the education they will require: Evidence from occupational forecasts', *Educational Researcher*, **20**, 2, pp. 11–20.

BALLE, F. (1991) 'The information society, schools and the media', in ERAUT, M. (Ed) *Education and the Information Society*, London, Cassell.

BARBER, B. (1984) *Strong Democracy*, Berkeley, University of California Press.

BARLOW, M. and ROBERTSON, H.-J. (1994) *Class Warfare*, Toronto, Key Porter.

BARMAN, H. and McCASKILL, D. (1986) *Indian Education in Canada*, Vancouver, University of British Columbia.

BARNETT, W.S. and ESCOBAR, C. (1987) 'The economics of early educational intervention: A review', *Review of Educational Research*, **57**, 4, pp. 387–414.

BARNHORST, R. and JOHNSON, L. (Eds) (1991) *The State of the Child in Ontario*, Toronto, Oxford University Press.

BASTIANI, J. (1995) *Working with Parents: A Whole School Approach*, London, Routledge.

BEARE, H. and BOYD, W.L. (Eds) (1993) *Restructuring Schools*, London, Falmer Press.

BENIGER, J. (1986) *The Control Revolution*, Cambridge, MA, Harvard University Press.

BERGER, P., BERGER, B. and KELLNER, H. (1973) *The Homeless Mind: Modernization and Consciousness*, New York, Random House.

BERLINER, D. and BIDDLE, B. (1995) *The Manufactured Crisis: Myth, Fraud, and the Attack on America's Public Schools*, New York, Addison Wesley.

BERRYMAN, S. (1992) 'Learning for the workplace', in DARLING HAMMOND, L. (Ed) *Review of Research in Education*, Washington, American Educational Research Association, Vol 19, pp. 343–401.

BOGDAN, R. and BIKLEN, S. (1982) *Qualitative Research for Education: An Introduction to Theory and Methods*, Boston, Allyn and Bacon.

BOLMAN, L. and DEAL, T. (1984) *Modern Approaches to Understanding and Managing Organizations*, San Francisco, Jossey-Bass.

BRACEY, G. (1996) 'The rhetoric versus the reality of job creation', *Phi Delta Kappan*, **77**, 5, pp. 385–6.

BRADSHAW, J. (1990) *Child Poverty and Deprivation in the UK*, London, National Children's Bureau.

BROWN, L.D. (1981) 'Participative research in a factory', in REASON, P. and ROWAN, J. (Eds) *Human Inquiry: A Sourcebook of New Paradigm Research*, Chichester, John Wiley, pp. 303–14.

BROWNING, D.S. (1991) *A Fundamental Practical Theology: Descriptive and Strategic Proposals*, Minneapolis, Fortress Press.

CANADIAN COUNCIL ON SOCIAL DEVELOPMENT (CCSD) (1992) Newletter #1 of the Centre for International Statistics on Economic and Social Welfare for Families and Children, Canadian Council on Social Development, June.

CANADIAN COUNCIL ON SOCIAL DEVELOPMENT (CCSD) (1993) Focus on child care, Newletter of the Centre for International Statistics on Economic and Social Welfare for Families and Children, Canadian Council on Social Development, July.

CIBULKA, J. (1996) 'The reform and survival of American public schools: An institutional perspective', in CROWSON, R., BOYD, W. and MAWHINNEY, H. (Eds) *The Politics of Education and the New Institutionalism: Reinventing the American School*, Washington, Falmer Press, pp. 7–22.

COHEN, D. (1987) 'Educational technology, policy, and practice', *Educational Evaluation and Policy Analysis*, **9**, 2, Summer, pp. 153–70.

COHEN, D. (1988) 'Educational technology and school organization', in NICKERSON, R. and ZODHIATES, P. (Eds) *Technology In Education: Looking Towards 2020*, Hillsdale, NJ, Lawrence Erlbaum, pp. 231–64.

COHEN, D. (1992) 'Policy and practice: The relations between governance and instruction', in GRANT, G. (Ed) *Review of Research in Education*, **18**, Washington, American Educational Research Association, pp. 3–49.

COHEN, D. (1995) 'What is the system in systemic reform?', *Educational Researcher*, **24/9**, pp. 11–17, 31.

COLEMAN, J. (1987) 'Families and schools', *Educational Researcher*, **16**, 6, pp. 32–8.

COLEMAN, P., COLLINGE, J. and TABIN, Y. (1995) 'The coproduction of learning: Improving schools from the inside out', in LEVIN, B., WALBERG, H. and FOWLER, W. (Eds) *Organizational Influences on Educational Productivity*, Greenwich, CT, JAI Press, pp. 141–74.

COMER, J. (1995) *School Power: Implications of an Intervention Project*, New York, Free Press.

CONNELL, R.W., WHITE, V.M. and JOHNSTON, K. (1991) *Running Twice as Hard: The Disadvantaged Schools Program in Australia*, Geelong, Deakin University Press.

References

CONWAY, J. (1993) *The Canadian Family in Crisis*, Toronto, James Lorimer.

COOLEY, W. and BICKEL, W. (1986) *Decision-oriented Educational Research*, Boston, Kluwer-Nijhoff.

CRESSY, G. (1994) 'Finding the common ground', in LAWTON, S., TOWNSEND, R. and TANENZAPF, E. (Eds) *Education and Community: The Collaborative Solution*, OISE, Toronto, pp. 137–47.

CROWSON, R., BOYD, W. and MAWHINNEY, H. (Eds) *The Politics of Education and the New Institutionalism: Reinventing the American School*, London, Falmer Press.

CUBAN, L. (1986) *Teachers and Machines: The Classroom Use of Technology Since 1920*, New York, Teachers College Press.

CUBAN, L. (1988) 'A fundamental puzzle of school reform', *Phi Delta Kappan*, **69**, 5, pp. 341–4.

CUBAN, L. (1990) 'Reforming again, again, and again', *Educational Researcher*, **19**, 1, pp. 3–13.

CULLINGFORD, C. (1991) *The Inner World of the School: Children's Ideas About Schools*, London, Cassell.

CUMMINS, J. (1988) *Minority Education: From Shame to Struggle*, Philadelphia, PA, Multilingual Matters.

DAVID, J. (1992) 'Realizing the promise of technology: The need for systemic education reform', Paper prepared for SRI International.

DE BRESSON, C. (1987) *Understanding Technological Change*, Montreal, Black Rose Books.

DENNISON, W. (1988) 'Education 2000: Trends, influences and constraints to the turn of the century', *Educational Management and Administration*, **16**, 1, pp. 33–42.

DEXTER, L. (1970) *Elite and Specialized Interviewing*, Chicago, Northwestern University Press.

DOUGLAS, M. (1986) *How Institutions Think*, Syracuse, NY, Syracuse University Press.

DROR, Y. (1986) *Policymaking Under Adversity*, New York, Transaction Books.

DRUCKER, P. (1992) *Managing for the Future*, New York, Truman Talley.

ECONOMIC COUNCIL OF CANADA (1992) *The New Face of Poverty: Income Security Needs of Canadian Families*, Ottawa, Minister of Supply and Services.

ELAM, S. and ROSE, L. (1995) 'The 27th Annual Phi Delta Kappan/Gallup Poll of the Public's Attitudes Towards the Public Schools', *Phi Delta Kappan*, **77**, 1, pp. 41–56.

ELMORE, R. (1992) 'Why restructuring alone won't improve teaching', *Educational Leadership*, **49**, 7, pp. 44–8.

ELSTER, J. (1983) *Sour Grapes: Studies in the Subversion of Rationality*, Cambridge, Cambridge University Press.

EMIHOVICH, C. (1990) 'Technocentrism revisited: Computer literacy as cultural capital', *Theory Into Practice*, **29**, 4, pp. 227–34.

EPSTEIN, J. (1995) 'School/family/community partnerships: Caring for the children we share', *Phi Delta Kappan*, **76**, 9, pp. 701–12.

FRIS, J. and BALDERSON, J. (1988) 'Leaders' priorities and the congruity imperative', *Alberta Journal of Educational Research*, **34**, 4, pp. 375–89.

FULLAN, M. (1991) *The New Meaning of Educational Change*, New York, Teachers College Press/ OISE Press.

GIDDENS, A. (1994) *Beyond Left and Right*, Cambridge, Polity Press.

GLEICK, J. (1987) *Chaos: The Making of a New Science*, New York, Viking.

GOODLAD, J. (1984) *A Place Called School*, New York, McGraw-Hill.

GRANT, G. and MURRAY, C. (1996) 'The second academic revolution', in CROWSON, R., BOYD, W. and MAWHINNEY, H. (Eds) *The Politics of Education and the New Institutionalism: Reinventing the American School*, London, Falmer Press, pp. 93–100.

GRUBB, N. (1996) 'The new vocationalism: What it is, what it could be', *Phi Delta Kappan*, **77**, 8, pp. 535–46.

GUBA, E. and LINCOLN, Y. (1981) *Effective Evaluation*, San Francisco, Jossey Bass.

GUNDERSON, M., MUSZYNSKI, L. and KECK, J. (1990) *Women and Labour Market Poverty*, Ottawa, Canadian Advisory Council on the Status of Women.

HABERMAN, M. (1991) 'The pedagogy of poverty versus good teaching', *Phi Delta Kappan*, **73**, 4, pp. 290–4.

HAIG-BROWN, C. (1988) *Resistance and Renewal: Surviving the Indian Residential School*, Vancouver, Tillacum Library.

HALPIN, D. (1996) 'Diversifying into the past or preparing for the millennium?: Comprehensive schooling for a post-traditional society', Address to the Department of Educational Studies, University of Oxford, 7 February.

HANDY, C. (1994) *The Empty Raincoat*, London, Random House.

HARGREAVES, A. (1994) *Changing Teachers, Changing Times*, New York, Teachers College Press.

HARGREAVES, A. (1995) 'Renewal in the age of paradox', *Educational Leadership*, **52**, 7, pp. 14–19.

HART, A. (1991) 'Leader succession and socialization: A synthesis', *Review of Educational Research*, **61**, 4, pp. 451–74

HENCHEY, N. (1988) 'Quality in Canadian public education: Some future perspectives', in STEVENSON, H. and WILSON, D. (Eds) *Quality in Canadian Public Education: A Critical Assessment*, London, Falmer Press, pp. 135–52.

HERMAN, R. and STRINGFIELD, S. (1995) 'Ten promising programs for educating disadvantaged students: Evidence of impact', Paper presented to the American Educational Research Association, San Francisco, April.

HOLMES, M. (1992) 'The revival of school administration: Alasdair MacIntyre in the aftermath of the common school', *Canadian Journal of Education*, **17**, pp. 422–36.

ILLICH, I. (1981) *Shadow Work*, Boston, M. Boyars.

KARWEIT, N. (1989) 'Effective preschool programs for students at risk', in SLAVIN, R., KARWEIT, N. and MADDEN, N. (Eds) *Effective Programs for Students at Risk*, Boston, Allyn and Bacon, pp. 75–102.

References

KAUFMAN, H. (1985) *Time, Chance and Organizations: Natural Selection in a Perilous Environment*, Chatham, NJ, Chatham House.

KIESLER, S. and SPROULL, L. (1982) 'Managerial response to changing environments: Perspectives on problem sensing from social cognition', *Administrative Science Quarterly*, **27**, pp. 548–70.

KNAPP, M., TURNBULL, B. and SHIELDS, P. (1990) 'New directions for educating the children of poverty', *Educational Leadership*, **48**, 1, pp. 4–8.

LEITHWOOD, K. (1992) 'The move toward transformational leadership', *Educational Leadership*, **49/5**, pp. 8–12.

LEITHWOOD, K., COUSINS, B. and SMITH, G. (1990) 'Principals' problem solving: Types of problems encountered', *Canadian School Executive*, **9/7**, pp. 9–12.

LEITHWOOD, K. and MENZIES, T. (1996) 'Forms and effects of school-based management: A review', Paper presented to the Canadian Society for the Study of Education, St. Catharines, ON.

LEVACIC, R. (1995) *Local Management of Schools: Analysis and Practice*, Buckingham, Open University Press.

LEVIN, B. (1986) 'The role of schools in preparation for work', *Western Economic Review*, **5/2**, pp. 72–83.

LEVIN, B. (1993) 'Collaborative research in and with organizations', *International Journal of Qualitative Studies in Education*, **6**, 4, pp. 331–40.

LEVIN, B. (1994) 'Education reform and the treatment of students in schools', *Journal of Educational Thought*, **28**, pp. 88–101.

LEVIN, B. (1995a) 'Education and poverty', *Canadian Journal of Education*, **20**, 2, pp. 211–24.

LEVIN, B. (1995b) 'How schools respond to a changing labour market', *Canadian Vocational Journal*, **30**, 3, pp. 8–20.

LEVIN, H. (1987) 'Accelerated schools for disadvantaged students', *Educational Leadership*, **44**, 6, pp. 19–21.

LEVITT, B. and MARCH, J. (1988) 'Organizational learning', *Annual Review of Sociology*, **14**, pp. 319–40.

LINDBLOM, C. (1990) *Inquiry and Change*, New Haven, Yale University Press, 1990.

LINDER, S. and PETERS, G. (1987) A design perspective on policy implementation', *Policy Studies Review*, **6/3**, pp. 459–75.

LISTON, D. (1988) *Capitalist Schools*, New York, Routledge.

LIVINGSTONE, D. (1985) 'Job skills and schooling: A class analysis of entry requirements and "overeducation"', in MASON, G. (Ed) *Transitions to Work*, Winnipeg, Institute for Social and Economic Research, University of Manitoba, pp. 106–29.

MACPHERSON, R.J.S. (1995) 'Educative accountability policy research: Methodology and epistemology', *Educational Administration Quarterly*, **32**, 1, pp. 80–106.

MACPHERSON, R.J.S. (1996) 'Accountability: Towards raising a "politically incorrect" issue', *Educational Management and Administration*, **23**, 4, pp. 139–50.

MADDEN, N., SLAVIN, R., KARWEIT, N., DOLAN, L. and WASIK, B. (1991) 'Success for all', *Phi Delta Kappan*, **72**, 8, pp. 593–9.

MAGSINO, R. (1991) 'The family: Parents' and students' rights', in GHOSH, R. and RAY, D. (Eds) *Social Change and Education in Canada*, Toronto, Harcourt Brace Jovanovich.

MARCH, J. (1984) 'How we talk and how we act: Administrative theory and administrative life', in SERGIOVANNI, T. and CORBALLY, J. (Eds) *Leadership and Organizational Culture*, Urbana, IL, University of Illinois Press, pp. 18–35.

MARCH, J. (1991) 'Exploration and exploitation in education', *Organizational Science*, **2/1**, pp. 71–87.

MARCH, J. and OLSEN, J. (1989) *Rediscovering Institutions*, New York, Free Press.

MAYNES, W. (1993) 'Child poverty in Canada: Challenges for educational policy-makers', *Canadian Review of Social Policy*, **32**, pp. 1–15.

McCALL, M. and KAPLAN, R. (1985) *Whatever It Takes: Decision Makers at Work*, Englewood Cliffs, Prentice-Hall.

McLAUGHLIN, M. (1987) 'Learning from experience: Lessons from policy implementation', *Educational Evaluation and Policy Analysis*, **9**, 2, pp. 171–8.

MERTTENS, R., NEWLAND, A. and WEBB, S. (1996) *Learning in Tandem: Involving Parents in Their Children's Education*, Leamington Spa, Scholastic.

MEYER, J. and ROWAN, B. (1977) 'Institutionalized organizations: Formal structure as myth and ceremony', *American Journal of Sociology*, **83/2**, pp. 340–63.

MEYER, M. and ZUCKER, L. (1989) *Permanently Failing Organizations*, Beverly Hills, CA, Sage.

MILES, M. and HUBERMAN, A. (1984) *Qualitative Data Analysis: A Sourcebook of New Methods*, Beverley Hills, CA, Sage.

MILLER, D. (1990) *The Icarus Paradox*, New York, Harper Collins.

MISHLER, E. (1986) *Research Interviewing: Context And Narrative*, Cambridge, Harvard University Press.

MJOKOWSKI, C. (1990) 'Developing technology applications for transforming curriculum and instruction', in WARGER, C. (Ed) *Technology in Today's Schools*, Alexandria, VA.

MULGAN, G. (1994) *Politics in an Antipolitical Age*, Cambridge, Polity Press.

NAISBITT, J. (1990) *Megatrends 2000: Ten New Directions for the 1990s*, New York, Morrow.

NATIONAL COUNCIL OF WELFARE (1992) *Poverty Profile, 1980–90*, Ottawa, The Council.

NATIONAL COUNCIL OF WELFARE (1993) *Poverty Profile Update for 1991*, Ottawa, The Council.

NATRIELLO, G., McDILL, E. and PALLAS, A. (1990) *Schooling Disadvantaged Children: Racing Against Catastrophe*, New York, Teachers College Press.

NETTLES, S. (1991) 'Community involvement and disadvantaged students: A review', *Review of Educational Research*, **61**, pp. 379–406.

References

Nickerson, R. (1988) 'Technology and education in 2020', in Nickerson, R. and Zodhiates, P. (Eds) *Technology in Education: Looking Towards 2020*, Hillsdale, NJ, Lawrence Erlbaum, pp. 1–9.

Nickerson, R. (1992) *Looking Ahead: Human Factor Challenges in a Changing World*, Hillsdale, NJ, Lawrence Erlbaum.

Nickerson, R. and Zodhiates, P. (1988) (Eds) *Technology in Education: Looking Towards 2020*, Hillsdale, NJ, Lawrence Erlbaum.

Noble, D. (1995) *Progress Without People*, Toronto, Between the Lines.

OECD (1993) *Education at a Glance*, Paris, CERI/OECD.

OECD (1995) 'Background Report to the Meeting of the Educational Committee at Ministerial Level, Chapter 1: Transitions to Learning Economies and Societies, OECD Document DEELSA/ED/MIN(96)2/ANN1, OECD, Paris.

Ogden, J. (1993) *The Last Book You'll Ever Read*, Toronto, Macfarlane Walter and Ross.

Olson, J. (1988) *Schoolworlds-Microworlds*, Oxford, Pergamon.

Osberg, L., Wien, F. and Grude, J. (1995) *Vanishing Jobs: Canada's Changing Workplace*, Toronto, James Lorimer.

Pacey, A. (1984) *The Culture of Technology*, Cambridge, MA, MIT Press.

Pfeffer, J. and Salancik, G. (1978) *The External Control of Organizations: A Resource Dependence Perspective*, New York, Harper and Row.

Plank, D. and Boyd, W.L. (1994) 'Antipolitics, education, and institutional choice: The flight from democracy', *American Educational Research Journal*, **31**, 2, pp. 263–81.

Powell, W. and Dimaggio, P. (1991) *The New Institutionalism in Organizational Analysis*, Chicago, University of Chicago Press.

Resnick, L. and Johnson, A. (1988) 'Intelligent machines for intelligent people: Cognitive theory and the future of computer-assisted learning', in Nickerson, R. and Zodhiates, P. (Eds) *Technology in Education: Looking Towards 2020*, Hillsdale, NJ, Lawrence Erlbaum.

Ricouer, P. (1981) *Hermeneutics and the Human Sciences*, Cambridge, Cambridge University Press.

Riffel, J.A. and Levin, B. (1986) 'Unsuccessful encounters: Teachers meet researchers in schools', *McGill Journal of Education*, **21**, 2, pp. 110–18.

Riffel, J.A. and Levin, B. (in press) 'Schools coping with the impact of information technology', *Educational Management and Administration*.

Riffel, J., Levin, B. and Young, J. (1996) 'Diversity in Canadian education', *Journal of Education Policy*, **11**, 1, pp. 113–23.

Roberts, K. (1995) *Youth and Employment in Modern Britain*, Oxford University Press.

Rubin, A. and Bruce, B. (1990) 'Alternate realizations of purpose in computer-supported writing', *Theory into Practice*, **29**, 4, Autumn, pp. 256–63.

Rudduck, J., Chaplain, R. and Wallace, G. (Eds) (1996) *School Improvement: What Can Pupils Tell Us?*, London, David Fulton.

Rumberger, R. (1987) 'The potential impact of technology on the skill requirements of future jobs in the United States', in Burke, G. and Rumberger, R.

(Eds) *The Future Impact of Technology on Work and Education*, London, Falmer Press.

SCHON, D. (1971) *Beyond the Stable State*, New York, W.W. Norton.

SEIDMAN, I. (1991) *Interviewing as Qualitative Research*, New York, Teachers College Press.

SENGE, P.M. (1990) *The Fifth Discipline: The Art and Practice of the Learning Organization*, New York, Doubleday/Currency.

SILVER, H. and SILVER, P. (1991) *An Educational War on Poverty*, Cambridge, Cambridge University Press.

SIMON, H. (1991) 'Bounded rationality and organizational learning', *Organizational Science*, **2**, 1, pp. 125–34.

SLAVIN, R. (1990) 'Research on cooperative learning: Consensus and controversy', *Educational Leadership*, **48**, 4, pp. 52–4.

SLAVIN, R., KARWEIT, N. and WASIK, B. (Eds) (1994) *Preventing Early School Failure*, Boston, Allyn and Bacon.

SLAVIN, R., MADDEN, N., KARWEIT, N., DOLAN, L., WASIK, B., ROSS, S. and SMITH, L. (1991) '"Whenever and wherever we choose . . .': The replication of success for all', *Phi Delta Kappan*, **75**, 8, pp. 639–47.

SMITH, T. and NOBLE, M. (1995) *Education Divides*, London, Child Poverty Action Group.

SNIDER, R. (1992) 'The machine in the classroom', *Phi Delta Kappan*, **74**, 4, pp. 316–23.

STAKE, R. (1988) 'Case study methods in educational research', in JAEGER, R. (Ed) *Complementary Methods for Research in Education*, Washington, American Educatonal Research Association.

STEIN, M.K., LEINHARDT, G. and BICKEL, W. (1989) 'Instructional issues for teaching students at risk', in SLAVIN, R., KARWEIT, N. and MADDEN, N. *Effective Programs for Students at Risk*, Boston, Allyn and Bacon, pp. 145–94.

STONE, D. (1988) *Policy Paradox and Political Reason*, Glenview, IL, Scott, Foresman.

TAYLOR, C. (1991) *The Malaise of Modernity*, Concord, ON, Anansi Press.

TESCH, R. (1990) *Qualitative Research: Analysis Types and Software Tools*, London, Falmer Press.

TIMAR, T. (1990) 'The politics of school restructuring', in MITCHELL, D. and GOERTZ, C. (Eds) *Education Politics for the New Century*, Bristol, PA, Falmer Press, pp. 55–74.

TINDER, G. (1991) *Political Thinking*, 5th Edition, New York, Harper Collins.

TOFFIER, A. and TOFFIER, H. (1995) *Creating a New Civilization: The Politics of the Third Wave*, Atlanta, Georgia, Turner Publishing, Inc.

TROYNA, B. (1993) *Racism and Education*, Philadelphia, Open University Press.

TYACK, D. and TOBIN, W. (1994) 'The "grammar" of schooling: What has it been so hard to change?', *American Educational Research Journal*, **31**, 3, pp. 453–79.

VAILL, P. (1989) *Managing as a Performing Art*, San Francisco, Jossey-Bass.

References

Vanier Institute of the Family (N.D.) *What Matters for Canadian Families?*, Ottawa, The Institute.

Walford, G. (Ed) (1991) *Doing Educational Research*, London, Routledge.

Warger, C. (Ed) (1990) *Technology in Today's Schools*, Alexandria, VA, ASCD.

Watkins, K. and Marswick, V. (1993) *Sculpting the Learning Organization: Lessons in the Art and Science of Systematic Change*, San Francisco, Jossey-Bass.

West, M. and Hopkins, D. (1995) 'Reconceptualising school effectiveness and school improvement', Paper presented to the European Conference on Educational Research, Bath, England, September.

White, M.A. (1990) 'A curriculum for the information age', in Warger, C. (Ed) *Technology in Today's Schools*, Alexandria, VA.

Williams, T. and Millinoff, H. (1990) *Canada's Schools: Report Card for the 1900s*, Toronto, Canadian Education Association.

Wilson, W.J. (1987) *The Truly Disadvantaged*, Chicago, University of Chicago Press.

Yin, R. (1989) *Case Study Research: Design and Methods*, Beverly Hills, Sage.

Zuboff, S. (1988) *In the Age of the Smart Machine: The Future of Work and Power*, New York, Basic Books.

Index